The Psalms

150 metrical Psalms for singing
to well-known hymn tunes

Martin E. Leckebusch

kevin mayhew

First published in 2006 by

KEVIN MAYHEW LTD
Buxhall, Stowmarket, Suffolk, IP14 3BW
E-mail: info@kevinmayhewltd.com
Web: www.kevinmayhew.com

9 8 7 6 5 4 3 2 1 0

ISBN 184417 515 4
Catalogue No 1500876

Cover design by Angela Selfe
Edited by Katherine Laidler
Typesetting by Fiona Connell Finch

Printed in Great Britain

Contents

Introduction

Psalms 1-150

Notes

Thematic index by psalm number

Metrical index by psalm number

Index of first lines and titles

With love to my daughters,

Rachel, Hannah, Abigail and Sarah

*'. . . bringing you delight and praise
throughout eternity.'*

Introduction

From a psalm to a hymn

It was a psalm that inspired the first hymn text I wrote. One morning I read Psalm 139 and felt the desire to *sing* it; and as I had to hand no songbook containing anything based on that psalm, I decided instead to try to write something from it which I could sing. The unexpected fruit of that day's devotional time was the first draft of the text which appears in this volume as *Through and through* – considerably amended, though recognisably based on that same original.

I have since discovered around 20 other hymns and songs from the same psalm, and in writing and rewriting psalm-based (and other) hymns I have learned a lot about both psalms and hymns, to say nothing of the process of writing hymns from the psalms. Psalm 139 turns out to have been a good place to start: though well known and in many ways straightforward, it nevertheless contains enough uncertainties and difficulties to highlight some of the questions which must be addressed when using the psalms in worship today.

Verses 1-6: Everything . . .

The emphasis of the opening section is that God is the God who sees and knows. This is a deep knowledge; the Psalmist is well aware that the whole of his life is under God's gaze. It is a direct knowledge, constantly changing as we live out our lives. It is an intimate knowledge, going beyond our movements (*sitting, rising, going out, lying down*); it penetrates just as easily to our motives (*you perceive my thoughts . . . you are familiar with all my ways*). The word *familiar* here seems to indicate constant attention to detail: God knows us well enough to recognise all our patterns of behaviour and thought and all our habits (good or bad!). Add to the picture the word *completely* (verse 4) and there are hints that from the perspective of eternity God sees the whole picture at once; verse 16 bears this out. Verse 4 also hints that God's knowledge of us is deeper than the self-knowledge which our generation prizes so highly. We may surprise ourselves by what we achieve or how we fail; we cannot surprise God. As Hagar said when her flight from Sarah's ill-treatment was halted by an encounter with the angel of the Lord: *You are the God who sees me . . . I have now seen the One who sees me* (Genesis 16:13).

Yet this may not be to our liking. To be known so intimately may be comforting – or daunting. *You hem me in*, says David (verse 5, New International Version*); You fence me round* (Jerusalem Bible), *You have beset me and shut me in* (Amplified Bible). There is almost a sense of menace here. Although the general tone so far is one of delight in God's loving acceptance, this may not be the writer's only emotion. What if the searching described here exposes our failures? Even more seriously, what if God's knowledge of our future is so powerful that it actually restrains our ability to choose how we live? *You have laid your hand upon me* – to guard and guide, or to control and constrain? There is a hint here of a kind of spiritual claustrophobia.

To be fair, it is only a hint. The interim conclusion reached in verse 6 is that God's understanding of us is wonderful; and while part of the reason is the sheer scale of something no human mind can fathom, the tenor of the psalm here indicates a believer who is glad to be known so fully. I have tried, in my first stanza, to capture this: the opening words (*My Lord*) are an echo of the intimacy implied here, as well as a deliberate avoidance of the more dated *O Lord* with which my first draft began. Disquiet at the enormity of God's knowledge of us is held over until the second stanza.

Nevertheless, the psalms do present to us some uncomfortable and challenging insights into God's nature and character. Here we are exposed to his awesome greatness, especially as Creator (for example, Psalms 8, 29, 46, 93, 96, 97, 104, 148). We are confronted with his burning holiness and the searching demands he makes on his people (Psalms 15, 24, 37, 39, 50, 51, 94); to balance this, we have plentiful reminders of his faithful commitment to us (Psalms 18, 34, 40, 66, 73, 91, 100, 107, 126, 132, 145). And lest we think this is all remote and mechanical, he offers us intimate closeness (Psalms 23, 84, 103, 116, 123, 130, 131, 139). This is the God of the Psalmists – a God who can be known, but never as fully as he knows us.

> O wondrous knowledge, awful might,
>
> unfathomed depth, unmeasured height![1]

Various writers have found inspiration in the encounter described in these opening verses. David Preston writes[2] how

> . . . every thought and deed lies open
>
> to your all-perceiving eyes;

---

1 *Lord, thou hast searched me, and dost know*: The Psalter Hymnal (1927)
2 *You, O Lord, have searched and known me*, David G. Preston (b.1949), © Author/Jubilate Hymns

He interprets verse 5 as 'guarded me before, behind'; but he, too, senses the implicit threat, and later says, 'from your grip I cannot stray'. Bernadette Farrell[3] captures the ambiguity of God's hand on us in a memorable phrase: 'with love everlasting you besiege me'; and, drawing on verse 11, 'Still I search for shelter from your light'. But for Peter Jarvis, verses 1-6 were sufficient: his text 'Lord, you have searched and known my ways[4] is drawn entirely from these verses. He writes:

> Caught in the compass of your mind
> are all the creatures you have made,

and his conclusion is,

> Enough that the Unsearchable
> has searched my heart and held my hand.

Verses 7-12: Anywhere . . .

The second section of the psalm picks up an earlier idea. *You perceive my thoughts from afar*, says the writer, and although so much of what he then says reveals the depth and intimacy of God's knowledge of him, it leaves open the question: how far? Can I travel such a distance that I am out of range of God's thoughts? Once again, too, there is the shadow of a desire to escape from the all-embracing cloak of being known by the infinite God: *Where can I go . . . ?* (verse 7).

Some Old Testament peoples envisaged their gods in territorial terms. When the Aramean Naaman, cleansed from leprosy, declared his new-found devotion to the God of Israel, he asked Elisha for a couple of mule-loads of earth to take back home, so that he could worship the Lord on – literally – Israelite soil (2 Kings 5:17).

Against this, the overwhelming witness of Law, Prophets and Writings is unanimous: the God of Israel is the Lord over all the earth, even over all creation. God may have chosen to reveal himself in special places on particular occasions, and Jerusalem may have been called his footstool; but Solomon wisely recognised that the temple he had just built could never contain God (1 Kings 8:27). It took exile far from Jerusalem to drive the lesson home to the nation as a whole.

These two ideas – the sovereignty of God and the notion that he was geographically limited – meet head-on in the paradox of Jonah, who was trying to run away from God by sailing to Tarshish (Jonah 1:3) yet had to confess that he worshipped *the Lord, the God of heaven, who made the sea and the land* (Jonah 1:9); and the book which bears his name ends with the prophet forcibly reminded that God cares for all peoples, Israelite or not.

---

3 *O God, you search me and you know me*, Bernadette Farrell (b.1957), © Author
4 *Lord, you have searched and known my ways*, Peter G. Jarvis (b.1925), © Author

> And if I take my flight into the dawn,
>
> or if I dwell on ocean's farthest shore,
>
> your mighty hand will rest upon me still,
>
> and your right hand will guard me evermore.

Thus runs Ian Pitt-Watson's paraphrase[5] of verses 9-10.

Small wonder, then, that the Psalmist finds his answer to be: there is *nowhere* I can escape God's presence, whether by height, depth or travelling across land and sea (verses 8-9). As Derek Kidner comments[6] on verse 8: 'The Gospel has given [it] a wholly new flavour, first in that Christ descended into Sheol on our behalf, and could not be held by it (Acts 2:24, 31), and secondly that for us Sheol has become Paradise. David's exclamation, *you are there!*, loses all its ambiguity with Paul's eager phrase, *With Christ, which is far better.*' Or as Rae E. Whitney has put it[7]:

> If I take the wings of morning,
>
> if to foreign lands I flee . . .
>
> There, O Love, I know you'll find me;
>
> there, O Love, I know you'll be,
>
> with Love's light you'll blind the darkness,
>
> with Love's life you'll rescue me.

Rae Whitney's text ranges far more widely than Psalm 139, but the lines quoted above touch on David's next theme: if distance cannot hide me from God, can darkness? Here the Psalmist puts his finger on a fundamental tendency of the human heart, the desire to shun the light (John 3:19-20). Yet it will not work: as my stanza 2 says, 'no darkness could conceal my path' – because the Light has shone in the darkness and the darkness has neither understood nor overcome it (John 1:5). Brian Foley expresses it beautifully[8]:

> If I should close my eyes to him
>
> he comes to give me sight;
>
> if I should go where all is dark,
>
> he makes my darkness light.

No darkness, whether external or internal, can extinguish the light of God.

5 *You are before me, Lord, you are behind*, Ian Robertson Pitt-Watson (1923-1995), © D. Pitt-Watson
6 Psalms 73-150: A commentary on books III-V of the Psalms, Derek Kidner, IVP, p. 465
7 *If I take the wings of morning*, Rae E. Whitney (b.1927), © Selah Publishing Co., Inc.
8 *There is no moment of my life*, William Brian Foley (1919-2000), © Faber Music Ltd

Stanza 2 of my text also reaches ahead to verse 16 and the question of time:

> The presence of your Spirit will
>
> be with me to the last.

Here, too, the perspective of the New Testament fulfils and enriches what is foreshadowed in the Old: *Never will I leave you; never will I forsake you.* (Hebrews 13:5, quoting Deuteronomy 31:6).

Verses 13-18: Always . . .

But before addressing the questions of time and eternity, the Psalmist voices another aspect of the theme: *It was you who created my inmost self* (verse 13, Jerusalem Bible). God made me, says the writer, and that is why and how he knows me; and he was active in my creation, not some passive spectator to the processes of biology. The implication of this verse seems to be that God shaped both my physical body (*you knit me together*) and my personality (*my inmost being*).

What is more, the thought emerges that before we were even conceived, God knew the span of our lives in the same awe-inspiring detail as everything else (verse 16). Other parts of the Old Testamant have more to say on this: for Jeremiah was clearly told (Jeremiah 1:5) that his calling as a prophet predated his own existence, implying that from that time God had been at work shaping him for the task. And if it was so for Jeremiah, why not for others, too, whose calling to share in God's purposes was written into the very fabric of their being? The New Testament is even clearer, with Paul assuring the Ephesians that they were hand-picked by God before the world's creation, a choice vindicated by their response to the Gospel and confirmed by the gift of the Spirit (Ephesians 1, especially verses 5, 13). As with verse 5, we may wonder whether this implies too much divine control and too little human freedom; but the Psalmist appears to have laid aside any lurking thoughts of being stifled by God, and is happy enough to enjoy security instead.

Is it merely that God has numbered our days? The sense of loving care kindled by such a thought yearns for more, and verse 18 hints at it. I have taken the words *when I awake, I am still with you* at face value:

> Before I sleep and as I wake
>
> I know that you are there,

which is both comforting and challenging in itself; but they also look beyond this life. The ending to Psalm 17 is similar, and certainly points to greater things; the two passages together undergird Paul's great hope, *then I shall know fully, even as I am fully known* (1 Corinthians 13:12).

This part of Psalm 139 does, however, raise another issue of concern to the hymnwriter: how to handle the advances brought by scientific research. David could speak of being *knit together* in the womb, though he had far less understanding than us of what that entailed. Nor is this the only psalm which is affected by such issues: further examples include Psalm 104:3-9, and Psalm 24:2. It seems to me that two principles can be invoked here to aid both understanding and hymn writing.

First, all truth is God's truth. Nothing which is true can be a denial of him, and advances in knowledge are fundamentally a good thing. (What is not so good is arrogantly to assume that we have enough science to know everything. Our understanding is still very limited, and the more we know, the more we should be awed by realising how little we really have understood.) Thus David's sense of wonder at how he was made in the womb is not negated by ultrasound scans: on the contrary, any parent who has seen their unborn child on the monitor will most likely have an even deeper sense of awe precisely because of their heightened awareness of what is happening!

The second principle is that science is science but poetry is poetry, and the two should be allowed to complement each other rather than trying to emulate or compete with each other. David wrote of the womb, but also of *the depths of the earth*, and nothing implies that he used the phrase literally. He employed metaphor to make his point, and it is a misunderstanding of literature to mistake this as rigorous scientific analysis.

This poetry is well reflected in Michael Hewlett's free paraphrase *O Lord, your all-perceiving eyes*[9], where verses 13-15 are linked with verse 2 to give a stanza which runs,

> You formed my limbs before they grew
> or found a shape to link them.
> You know my body through and through,
> *my thoughts before I think them.*

Michael Saward[10], too, mingles the literal and the metaphorical:

> Every inch of flesh and sinew,
> every blood cell, every bone . . .
> you have fashioned me and formed me,
> shaped and spun me, watched me grow . . .

9 *O Lord, your all-perceiving eyes*, Michael Hewlett (1916-2000), © Mrs Rachel Belringer
10 *Lord, you've tested me and known me*, Michael Saward (b.1932), © Author / Jubilate Hymns

As the Psalmist looks at himself in these verses he is amazed by what he finds – how much God thinks about him! What intimacy, what commitment are implied in this depth of knowledge! Yet whereas we might easily – almost instinctively – respond to this by concluding that *we* are wonderful and special, David's reaction (verses 17-18) is neither self-satisfaction nor self-absorption but God-centred awe. This is worship founded on truth, explored with delight rather than whittled down to some bland repetition; it is worship focused on God and *his* deeds rather than being caught up in *my* experiences and feelings.

Verses 19-24: Honestly?

Then comes the sting in the tail. The sharp outburst of verses 19-22 is not without parallel in the Psalms, but it seems particularly at odds with the gentleness of the previous verses. At one level, it looks like no more than sheer vitriol; even if we see it as zealous rage, David's eagerness to express hatred towards those who do not share his faith makes for uncomfortable reading. In addition, what are we to make of the final two verses? Is this naïve self-justification after the previous diatribe, or is there anything more profound here?

The wider question, of course, is how we are to deal with these uncongenial elements in the Psalter. Psalms 2, 34, 41, 62, 63, 79 and 110 all contain stern warnings of divine judgement; Psalms 69, 109 and 137, like 139, go even further. Are we to discard them as sub-standard, sub-Christian and unworthy of inclusion in the Bible? To do so not only challenges the authority of Scripture in a way which many believers will find unacceptable; it also undermines the integrity of the texts. The Psalms have reached us as complete units, and in the first case this is surely how we should try to understand them. Better than to discard them is to read and reassess them in the light of the Gospel. Many of the psalms bear witness to a level of suffering that we have not experienced, although it is still not uncommon for Christians; and, sadly, the cries of pain and yearnings for justice and deliverance which these writers expressed were never more relevant or urgent than today. More-over, in the words of Psalms we find real people expressing real feelings; all those people and some of their outbursts were sinful, but few of them are worse than any of us have felt on occasions. In all these ways, their words still have things to say into the context of corporate worship, and the Church ignores these dimensions to its loss.

As for the task of creating new songs from specific psalms, there are many solutions. Bernadette Farrell's text from this psalm, quoted above[11], does not venture beyond verse 18; nor does Dan Schutte's 'Yahweh, I know you are near'[12]. Gerard Markland omits verses 19-22 but includes verses 23-24 in his song 'Father God, gentle Father God'[13].

At the other extreme, Michael Saward[14] and David Preston[15] both stay close to the original text, the latter saying,

> . . . judge the wicked,
>
> break their blasphemous design!
>
> How can I not hate such evil?
>
> Lord, your enemies are mine

while the former writes,

> All who crush the course of justice,
>
> how I loathe such evil men!

Both these hymn writers capture David's feelings of indignation – not personal vindictiveness, but a deep concern for God's glory.

Isaac Watts even wrote a whole text[16] from these final verses of Psalm 139, rendering verse 21 as

> does not my soul detest and hate
>
> the sons of malice and deceit?

Moving on to the final two verses of the psalm, Watts continues:

> Lord, search my soul, try every thought;
>
> though my own heart accuse me not
>
> of walking in a false disguise,
>
> I beg the trial of thine eyes.

The psalm's conclusion is not empty bluster; it is an honest opening of a heart to God.

Why did David include the rage of verses 19-22? If I had written this psalm, I would have erased those verses when I realised how violent they were. But to do so would have covered up what was in my heart, which seems out of place in a psalm celebrating God's complete knowledge and total acceptance of us. To leave the outburst as part of the psalm, and then conclude with a deliberate submission to God's searchlight, is far more honest. Hence my more tempered final stanza, with its closing lines:

---

11 *O God, you search me and you know me*, Bernadette Farrell (b.1957), © Author
12 *Yahweh, I know you are near*, Daniel L. Schutte (b.1947), © Author
13 *Father God, gentle Father God*, Gerard Markland (b.1953), © Kevin Mayhew Ltd
14 *Lord, you've tested me and known me*, Michael Saward (b.1932), © Author/Jubilate Hymns
15 *You, O Lord, have searched and known me*, David G. Preston (b.1949), © Author/Jubilate Hymns
16 *My God, what inward grief I feel*, Isaac Watts (1674-1748)

so search me, Lord, and cleanse my heart
from all that you abhor,
then teach me how to walk with you
today and evermore.

Finally

It is now nearly two decades since I penned that initial draft of 'My Lord, you have examined me'. In the intervening years, hymn writing has become a significant part of my life; through it I have made numerous friends, and many of them have inspired and taught me, often by their own writing. So, too, have friends made in other ways. Above all, my wife, Jane, continues to encourage and support me. The project to produce a text on each of the psalms has occupied almost five years, and has brought its own challenges and delights; and my thanks are due to all who have helped to make this book a reality.

These texts are offered firstly to the Lord, Father, Son and Holy Spirit, to whom the Psalms – like the rest of the Scriptures – bear witness; and then they are offered to Christ's Church, in the hope that they will help some of my brothers and sisters to encounter the psalms afresh, and to take up the songs of our heritage in today's world. I also hope that they will play a part in unlocking those same riches for a new generation; not least my daughters, Rachel, Hannah, Abigail and Sarah, all born since that first draft was written. They know that I treasure hymns; I also treasure them, and it is with love that I dedicate this volume to them.

Martin E. Leckebusch

The finest fruit

A depth of satisfaction:
the promise is made known
to all who turn from evil
and make the Lord their own;
    who heed no wicked counsel,
    no cynic's mocking voice;
    whose way of living signals
    obedience as their choice.

The man or woman choosing
to follow what is right
will find God's word becoming
a source of pure delight:
    here meditation causes
    the finest fruit to grow
    as when a tree is planted
    where streams of water flow.

To trust in God will give us
a grounding firm and sure;
to disregard his wisdom
would make us insecure;
    Lord, let us not be worthless
    like chaff that blows away –
    but guide us and protect us;
    watch over us each day.

Metre: **76 76 D**
Crüger (Herrnhut); Ellacombe;
Jacaranda (Rosalie Bonighton)

Give honour to the Son

Why do the nations rage
against God's righteous reign,
assuming that the law
is some restrictive chain?
   Enthroned on high,
   God hears their cry –
and knows their threats are all in vain.

For by divine decree
heaven's purpose is made known:
God's one and only Son
now sits on Zion's throne;
   his many foes
   he overthrows,
and claims the nations as his own.

Give honour to the Son:
be wise, and seek his face,
for those who spurn God's law
risk judgement and disgrace –
   so come, draw near
   in reverent fear,
and he will be your hiding-place.

Metre: **66 66 44 8**
Gopsal

You are my security

When the pressures I encounter
cause a sense of real alarm,
when the people closest to me
side with those who wish me harm,
rumours fly – can it be
that you might abandon me?

Lord, I know: in all my troubles
you are my security;
when I feel ashamed and worthless,
grace restores my dignity.
Why should I feel despair,
trusting you to hear my prayer?

Peace is mine, though danger threatens;
sleep, however dark the night;
strength to face the new day's challenge
as I meet the morning light.
Countless foes may loom near;
safe in you, I need not fear.

Lord, arise, my strong Deliverer;
keep ungodly powers at bay.
You who silence wicked schemers,
spare me in the evil day;
then with heaven's very best
may your people's lives be blessed!

Metre: **87 87 67**
Michael

Guide my thoughts tonight

Have mercy, Righteous One,
and listen as I pray:
God, answer me as I unload
the burdens of the day.

Though many spurn your voice,
embracing lies and shame,
yet those you choose to walk with you
are called, each one by name.

Should anger turn my mind
to brooding, vengeful spite?
My heart is yours to search and rule:
Lord, guide my thoughts tonight.

And when despair looms large,
I yearn to glimpse your face –
how pallid this world's treasures seem
beside the joys of grace!

To shelter in your care:
this choice, Lord, I have made;
so keep me safe the whole night through,
asleep and unafraid.

Metre: **66 86 (SM)**
Sandys

A welcome guest

My God, I pray for help:
each morning hears me sigh
as still I wait expectantly
for your reply.

You are the Holy One
who cannot tolerate
our pride, our lies, our bitterness –
such things you hate.

When warlike hearts erupt
in venom freely poured,
will you not mark each guilty tongue
for judgement, Lord?

Yet to your house I come,
a welcome guest by grace,
to worship you, to learn your will,
to seek your face.

To those who love your name
your favour is revealed;
let all who trust you find in you
their joy and shield.

Metre: **66 84**
Swyncombe (John Barnard); Amen Court

Not in anger

Not in anger but in love
answer my impassioned plea:
how long till you free my soul
from this gnawing agony?

Grievous sorrow weighs me down;
conflict often mars my days;
tears of anguish fill my nights –
spare my life to sing your praise.

Though confronted by my foes,
mine is triumph, not despair;
Lord, your mercy never fails:
you have not ignored my prayer!

Metre: **77 77**
Ephraim

Inclusive language variation
3.3 God whose mercy never fails,

Yours is the verdict

You are my Refuge and Deliverer,
my only shelter from the fight;
merciless enemies pursue me,
forcing me headlong into flight.
Yet these accusers, these assailants –
may they secure my downfall, Lord,
if I have disregarded justice,
if I have soiled my hands with fraud.

Rise up, my God, in holy anger:
counter the spite my foes have shown;
gather the nations in your presence;
make your unerring judgements known.
Grant me and all your people safety;
guard us from those who love to hate;
you probe each mind and every conscience:
yours is the verdict we await.

You are my Shield, my Judge, my Saviour,
upholding justice every day;
those who will not repent of evil
you will be ready to repay:
would not my just reward be trouble
if making trouble were my aim?
Thankful that you are always righteous,
I lift my praises to your name.

Metre: **98 98 D**
Rendez à Dieu

A hallmark and a signature

Your majesty is splendid, Lord,
surpassing all that you have made –
a hallmark and a signature,
throughout the universe displayed.

To children you reveal delights
unseen by jaded adult eyes –
how eagerly they sound your praise,
enthralled by every new surprise.

And when we pause to contemplate
the vastness of the galaxy,
in hushed amazement we recall
how you enfold us constantly.

For we enjoy an honoured place,
confirming our eternal worth:
exalted over birds and beasts,
and charged to care for all the earth.

A hallmark and a signature
throughout the universe displayed –
your majesty is splendid, Lord,
surpassing all that you have made!

Metre: **88 88 (LM)**
Gonfalon Royal; Bow Brickhill;
Blakesley Hall (Andrew Fletcher)

Extol the God of justice
with heart and soul and voice;
remember all his wonders,
recount them and rejoice.
He stands with all who labour
for what is true and right,
till wickedness and falsehood
are banished from his sight.

Extol the God of justice
enthroned for evermore,
a stronghold in affliction,
a refuge to the poor:
he hears the cries of victims
and senses their despair;
in faithfulness he honours
the faith that sparks our prayer.

Extol the God of justice,
however dark the day:
the hope that calls for mercy
will not be turned away;
for evil shall not triumph,
nor human sin prevail:
the Lord is God eternal,
whose judgements cannot fail.

Metre: **76 76 D**
Wolvercote

Inclusive language variations
1.3   remember bygone wonders,
1.5   God stands with all who labour
1.8   are banished far from sight.
2.5   who hears the cries of victims
2.7   whose faithfulness will honour

10 When trouble looms

When trouble looms on every side,
when conflict dominates the day,
when life presents no easy path,
    Lord, why do you seem far away?

From every plan which harms the poor,
from schemes to victimise the weak,
from those who snare the innocent,
    Lord, your defence, your help we seek.

The greed which never has enough,
the boasts of haughty insolence,
the words which threaten, lie or curse –
    Lord, keep us from such arrogance.

Some think that you are blind to sin;
some live as though you were not there;
some treat your justice with contempt;
    Lord, surely you both see and care!

You call the wicked to account;
you champion the victims' cause;
you silence mortal taunts and threats;
    Lord, heaven's eternal throne is yours.

Metre: **88 88 (LM)**
Winchester New

My refuge is God

My refuge is God: why, then, should I flee,
though numerous threats are ranged against me?
So much looks imperilled by such an attack,
but God is my refuge – why should I shrink back?

From heaven's lofty throne the Lord sees each heart:
the good and the bad, he tells them apart.
The right and the wrong we embrace or forsake –
his judgements take shape on the choices we make.

When troubles abound, in God I will trust,
the Righteous and True, the Faithful and Just;
though wickedness leads to unending disgrace,
the upright will meet with the Lord face to face.

Metre: **10 10 11 11**
Hanover

Inclusive language variations
2.1-2   From heaven's lofty throne our God sees
          each heart,
          the good and the bad, and tells them apart.
2.4   what judgements take shape on the choices
          we make!

Words that only wound

A patchwork quilt of platitudes and lies:
so much of what is said amounts to this!
Lord, help: for godly tongues are seldom heard,
and so few grieve that this is how it is.

The words that trumpet minor trophies gained;
the echoes from the caverns of deceit;
the twisted truth that charms the hearer's heart –
when judged by you, their silence is complete.

Will you not rise and speak in the defence
of those oppressed by falsehood, or maligned?
Are your words not the cornerstone of truth,
and pure as silver seven times refined?

When arrogance is treated with respect,
when cynicism finds an honoured place,
preserve us, Lord, from words that only wound,
and keep us from the counsels of disgrace.

Metre: **10 10 10 10**
West Ashton (John Barnard)

Unless you help me

When anxious thoughts assail my mind,
when I begin to doubt your care,
when gloom and sorrow flood my soul,
I bring my fears to you, my God, in prayer.

I call to you to answer soon,
to turn my darkness into light,
for life can be a battlefield –
unless you help me, I shall lose the fight!

Yet in your endless love I trust,
in your salvation I rejoice:
because you have been good to me
I offer you my praise with heart and voice.

Metre: **8 8 8 10**
Bardfield Sailing (Ian Sharp);
Jasmine (Rosalie Bonighton)

14   If only

If I should close my heart of hearts,
Lord God, to thoughts of you,
what lurking evils deep within
might taint the things I do?

If you subject this sinful world
to your all-seeing gaze,
how many people do you find
who long to know your ways?

If evil schemers harm the weak,
is your response not clear?
You shield the poor in troubled times;
the righteous find you near.

If only, Lord, you would make real
what Zion seldom knows:
rekindled hearts, and lives restored,
and joy which overflows.

Metre: **86 86 (CM)**
Irish

Lord, I approach your sanctuary –
but as I come to seek your face
the challenges of holiness
confront me in this sacred place.

Your searchlight falls across my path –
what flaws and failures will it show?
Am I content to speak the truth,
to slander neither friend nor foe?

Esteem for those who savour sin,
disdain for those who fear your name –
Lord, if such attitudes are mine,
then I deserve to suffer shame.

If I neglect some costly pledge,
or let a bribe distort my sight,
or simply disregard the poor –
convict me, Lord, of wrong and right.

Give me a single-minded faith,
an eager ear for your command;
make mine a life securely built
on solid rock, not shifting sand.

Metre: **88 88 (LM)**
Fulda; Wylde Green (Andrew Fletcher)

God before me, God beside me

God beyond earth's finest treasures,
you alone shall have my praise;
I will love your cherished people,
I will serve you all my days;
    be my ruler,
    be my refuge,
God the guardian of my ways.

You have caused my life to prosper –
countless gifts your love has planned!
Day and night your wisdom prompts me,
shows me all that you command;
    God before me,
    God beside me,
safe within your care I stand.

When my earthly days are over,
fresh delights remain in store:
vaster riches, fuller pleasures
than I ever knew before –
    life unending,
    joy unfading
in your presence evermore.

Metre: **87 87 447**
Praise my Soul (Steve James); Walden (Richard Lloyd)

I bring my prayer

From a well-intentioned heart
open to your scrutiny,
from a soul that shuns deceit,
valuing integrity,
Lord, I bring my prayer to you,
choosing words I know are true.

Wondrous love, unfailing power –
what delights your kindness brings!
Let me find security
in the shelter of your wings
when my foes are all around,
keen to throw me to the ground.

Guard me from such enemies;
halt them with your firm rebuff.
Grant me peace and all I need,
for your care is wealth enough
till, perfected by your grace,
I awake to see your face.

Metre: **77 77 77**
Heathlands

Inclusive language variation
1.5   God, I bring my prayer to you,

Refuge and Rock

Refuge and Rock, Shield and Deliverer!
I love you, Lord, for your unfailing care:
facing the grave, fearing destruction,
I called to you and you answered my prayer:
I was distressed – you heard my voice;
I will rejoice in your salvation.

Earthquake and fire, thunder and lightning!
Clothed in such armour you sprang to my aid;
parting the heavens, bursting with splendour,
you left your foes overwhelmed and dismayed.
Your awesome power, your tender grace
gave me a place where I could flourish.

Faithful and pure, blameless and perfect –
yet to the crooked you show yourself shrewd.
Your holy light shines on my darkness;
my steps are guided, my vigour renewed.
Your law will shape my heart and mind,
letting me find your richest blessing.

Wisdom and strength, honour and triumph!
Such are the gifts you are eager to give:
strength for the fight; wisdom to lead me;
triumph and more for as long as I live;
honour indeed to make it known
that you alone are God Eternal.

Worship and thanks, reverence and glory
be to the Lord I am honoured to know;
saved from my foes, called to your service,
I will extol you wherever I go.
Your love surrounds me all my days:
therefore I praise you, God, my Saviour.

Metre: **9 10 9 10 8 9**
Earth and All Stars

The heavens proclaim God's glory,
the skies sing out in praise,
extolling their creator
through endless nights and days.
More eloquent than language,
more radiant than the sun,
this message of God's splendour
is meant for everyone.

The law of God is perfect,
its precepts always right,
revealing timeless wisdom,
providing life and light –
no gold could be so precious,
no honey taste as sweet;
and those who yield obedience
will find their joy complete.

Forgive my secret failures,
the faults I do not know;
from wilful sins protect me,
and ways I should not go.
May all my meditations,
my every thought and word,
be fashioned for your pleasure,
my Saviour and my Lord.

Metre: **76 76 D**
St Theodulph; Splendour (John Marsh)

Help in troubled times

For help in troubled times we pray,
for grace when life is hard,
and for the presence of our God
to comfort, guide and guard.

We ask the bounty of success
on every right desire,
aware that God sees all the heights
to which our thoughts aspire.

If human skill was all we had,
how swiftly we would fall;
our only hope is in the Lord,
who answers when we call.

The best resources this world gives
will fail, decay or rust;
the God of heaven has endless strength –
in him alone we trust.

Metre: **86 86 (CM)**
Wiltshire; Everard (John Jordan)

Your gifts exceed
whatever we could ask, and all we need:
Lord, you have answered prayer
with peace that conquers strife,
with greater wealth than gold,
with everlasting life:
yes, what can move
the saints who choose to trust your endless love?

For your delight
we praise your holiness and sing your might:
can wickedness survive
your all-consuming flame?
Will sin not be exposed
to everlasting shame?
When you draw near,
the powers that scorn your reign will disappear.

Metre: **4 10 6 6 6 6 4 10**
Luckington

Inclusive language variation
1.3   for you have answered prayer

The lonely sufferer

Lord, hear the lonely sufferer's cry:
'Why, God, have you forsaken me?
Why does your silence fill my ears
though I pursue you fervently?
    For are you not the Holy One
    enthroned in timeless splendour,
    the One whose aid our forebears knew,
    their Refuge and Defender?'

Denied the joy of self-respect,
beset by those who doubt your care,
Lord, who could quell the anxious thoughts
which pave the pathways of despair?
    But still your lifelong call remains,
    through testing times enduring –
    come, faithful God, your promise prove,
    the sufferer's hope restoring.

With strength and courage ebbing fast,
with fierce opponents close at hand,
with life itself about to end
this sufferer prays for grace to stand:
    'Come swiftly, Lord! I need your help –
    aggressive foes assail me!
    Be nearer than the threats I dread –
    I trust you not to fail me!'

Lord, hear the joyful sufferer's cry –
the cry of faith refined and strong
from one who tells of answered prayer,
inviting all to join the song:
    so may your worship, gracious God,
    resound through all the nations,
    to publicise your righteousness
    to future generations.

Metre: **88 88 87 87**
Fernhurst (Colin Mawby)

Within the busy rush of life
    I find a resting-place:
when I submit to Christ my Lord
    and let him set my pace
he shows the way that I should take
    whatever trials I face.

Amid the choices I must make
    and duties that increase
he comes to calm my anxious thoughts,
    to make the turmoil cease;
as in his presence I remain
    he guides me into peace.

The timeless, all-sufficient God
    my every longing knows
and daily he refreshes me
    with joy which overflows;
anointed by tranquillity
    my strength to serve him grows.

My Saviour bids me walk with him
    and follow all his ways –
his plan for me is fruitfulness
    throughout my earthly days,
since now and evermore I live
    beneath his loving gaze.

Metre: **86 86 86**
Morden; Brother James' Air; St Silas; Raydale;
Cray (Richard Lloyd)

The glorious King

Let every door be opened wide:
the Lord returns, his battles done –
he takes his throne, the glorious King,
by whom the fiercest fight was won.

His realm extends to all he made:
the earth; the riches it contains;
the heights and depths of human life –
throughout the universe he reigns.

But in his presence who can stand?
Who dares to seek his holy face?
How can our hearts and hands be pure
but by his favour and his grace?

Let every heart be opened wide:
our Lord returns, his battles done –
he takes his throne, our glorious King,
whose gracious reign has now begun.

Metre: **88 88 (LM)**
Gonfalon Royal; Truro; Agincourt;
Porta (Andrew Moore)

I gladly trust

Lord, I gladly trust in you:
let me not be put to shame.
    As I look towards your throne
    make your gracious promise known:
God my refuge and my hope,
your protective care I claim.

In your hands I place my past:
all my sins you know so well.
    Your forgiveness, Lord, I need,
    for my guilt is great indeed;
even greater is your love –
mercy more than I can tell.

Teach me what is true and good;
let me hear and understand!
    In the choices I must make
    show my heart the way to take,
so that I may always tread
on the path which you have planned.

When my troubles multiply
you alone can bring me through:
    so with all your saints I say,
    'Be my strength and shield today.'
Since I know you hear my prayer,
Lord, I gladly trust in you.

Metre: **77 77 77**
Petra; Ratisbon; Mysia (June Nixon)

A blameless life

A steadfast heart, a blameless life:
may these be my gift, Lord, to you,
with faith and love and truthfulness
expressed in all I do.

To shun deceit and wickedness,
be this the choice I always make;
the counsel of hypocrisy
I willingly forsake.

Be clean my hands and pure my heart
when to your holy house I come;
your matchless deeds be all my song,
your presence be my home.

The schemes of those who kill for wealth –
let such be never mine to share;
your mercy be sufficient, Lord,
whatever guilt I bear.

A steadfast heart, a blameless life:
may this be your work, Lord, in me,
until I sing, with all the saints,
your praise eternally.

Metre: **88 86**
Saffron Walden; Daphne (Alan Viner)

My chosen home

With God my Saviour as my light,
why should I be afraid?
The fiercest foes who threaten me
will find me undismayed.

God's temple is my chosen home;
his beauty draws my gaze –
though troubles rage on every side
my heart still flows with praise.

The focus of my prayer is this:
that I may see his face,
and prove his mercy more than plumbs
the depths of my disgrace.

And should my very family
acknowledge me no more,
the Lord remains my hiding-place –
in him I rest secure.

So when I find myself at risk
from lurking treachery,
Lord, show me how to walk with you
in full integrity.

For this I know: throughout my life
your love will hold me fast –
and I shall trust and hope in you
from this day to my last.

Metre: **86 86 (CM)**
Westminster; Waveney (Betty Roe)

I call to you, my Rock:
Lord, hear my earnest prayer –
if you ignore my plea
how can I not despair?
As I reach out, make this the place
of fresh encounters with your grace.

May I be spared the fate
of those who cling to sin,
whose friendly words belie
malicious thoughts within –
would ruin not be my reward
if I should disregard you, Lord?

But you have heard my prayer,
and you will make me strong:
since I rely on you
my heart is filled with song,
for you, Lord, are my sanctuary,
your people's hope eternally.

Metre: **66 66 88**
St John (Adoration); Earlsdon (Michael Higgins)

The voice

The voice which shakes the earth
till mountains heave and quake,
the voice which causes ancient oaks
    to bend and break,
the voice which thunders loud
above the crashing waves
belongs to God, the Holy One,
    the Lord who saves.

When God's majestic voice
round hill and valley rings,
the desert blooms, the woodland skips,
    the forest sings:
his word proclaims the truth
like lightning, sharp and bright,
with penetrating clarity
    and tender might.

At his eternal throne
await the solemn sound,
for nowhere else will greater strength
    or peace be found.
Exalt the God of power,
and kneel in reverent fear –
give glory to the One whose voice
    we long to hear.

Metre: **66 84 D**
Leoni; Ancient Oak (Simon Clark)

Inclusive language variations
2.5   For here are words of truth
3.1   Approach the maker's throne,

Both extremes

I will sing your mercies, Lord,
how you heard and answered prayer:
foes disarmed and fears relieved –
you have lifted my despair.

Your displeasure swiftly fades,
even when your anger burns;
though the night is full of tears,
with the dawn our joy returns.

I have tasted both extremes,
confidence and deep dismay:
from your strength, security;
from your silence, disarray.

In profound distress I prayed:
'Gracious God, prolong my days –
can the grave extol your name?
Let me live, and sing your praise!'

Then my grief was turned to joy;
then my laughter was restored –
one unending song of thanks
I will bring to you, my Lord.

Metre: **77 77**
Emma; Ephraim; Swaledale (Stanley Vann)

My Rock and my Refuge, take note of my cry;
my Strength and my Saviour, on you I rely.
My righteous Deliverer, preserve me from shame –
may I know your guidance, and honour your name.

What power can dissuade me from trusting in you?
My heart will be yours, for I know you are true!
My soul was imprisoned till you set me free;
I bask in the love you have lavished on me.

But now I am troubled, and fear for my life;
my days are a pageant of sorrow and strife:
for slander surrounds me, and terror looms near –
my neighbours deride me, my friends disappear.

My welfare and future to you I entrust –
protect me from those whose designs are unjust.
Lord, purge from creation all falsehood and spite;
enable your servants to live in your light.

Such total protection, such answers to prayer –
may all who revere you rejoice in your care!
Take courage, you saints, and be strong in the Lord,
for he is your Hope, your eternal Reward.

Metre: **11 11 11 11**
Datchet; St Denio; Tintern (Robert Jones)

The thrill of God's forgiveness
is more than words can tell –
a peace that comes from pardon,
a sense that all is well:
for those who treat their failures
with candour, not deceit,
will find in God's acceptance
their joy is made complete.

How often we are silent
when sin should be confessed:
we quash the Spirit's prompting
and rob our souls of rest;
but when our lips acknowledge
the wrongs that we have done,
our peace is reinstated,
our guilty load is gone.

Let all whose deepest yearnings
are shown by godly lives
draw daily on God's mercy
until the Day arrives:
for in that final judgement
which settles right and wrong
the Lord will be our refuge,
his saving power, our song.

Lord, may we not be stubborn,
or slow to understand
your Spirit's patient counsel,
your steady guiding hand;
however life may treat us,
your love will bring us through –
with all who know your mercy
we will rejoice in you.

Metre: **76 76 D**
Thornbury; Hadley (Andrew Wright)

Inclusive language variation
3.8   the Saviour's power, our song.

Be joyful, be skilful, and come with new songs –
give praise to the Lord, for to him it belongs!

In all things the Lord is proved faithful and right,
for justice and holiness are his delight.

Revere him whose word set the oceans in place,
whose voice sent the stars on their journeys through
    space.

Through all generations his purpose will stand –
his will overrules what the nations have planned.

Each heart he examines, our secrets are known;
how happy we are – still he makes us his own!

Though earthly resources are powerless to save,
trust him, and no longer need you fear the grave.

In you, Lord, we hope, and on you we depend:
may love rest upon us – your love without end.

Metre: **11 11**
Rainforest (Rosalie Bonighton)

I will praise the Lord for ever,
such a tale is mine to tell;
those who hear of my deliverance,
let them join the song as well.
He released me from my troubles
when I called to him by name;
those who trust in God are radiant –
what can turn their joy to shame?

See how love's attentive kindness
sounds the death-knell of our fear;
when our problems overwhelm us,
God will send his angels near.
Praise the Lord, who heals his people,
making wounded spirits whole,
for he understands the anguish
that can pierce the human soul.

Praise the Lord, whose heart for justice
leads the righteous on their way,
while for those intent on evil
he reserves a judgement day:
if we long for God's approval
as the crown of all we do,
let the truth become our watchword,
peace, the vision we pursue.

Who could count a lifetime's trials?
He will guide us through them all;
safe in his eternal keeping,
we are rescued if we fall.
God's protection never falters;
whose provision rivals his?
Trust and praise the Lord for ever;
taste and see how good he is!

Metre: **87 87 D**
Ode to Joy

Take up your servants' cause, Lord,
and be your people's shield:
defend them from the weapons
their persecutors wield.
May schemes to vex believers
collapse in disarray –
despatch protecting angels
to sweep such plans away.

Those saints treat their oppressors
with unexpected care:
they make their foes' misfortunes
a spur to earnest prayer.
Now may the ruthless probing
believers have to face
rebound on the accusers,
exposing their disgrace.

The faithful brave an onslaught
of malice without cause,
while many mock their hardships
with laughter and applause;
your people's lives are threatened
by lions fierce and strong –
come swiftly, Lord, to save them;
restore their hope, their song.

Contend, Lord, for your people;
take up your servants' fight;
discomfit those who treat them
with arrogance and spite.
Announce the vindication
your children long to see –
then all your saints will praise you
throughout eternity.

Metre: **76 76 D**
Aurelia

Wisdom whispers

Wisdom whispers in my heart,
gives me honest words to say,
urges me to shun deceit,
points me to the better way,
probes and punctures vanity,
warns me not to compromise,
keeps the need for holy fear
constantly before my eyes.

Righteousness like mountain peaks;
kindness as the heavens above;
justice deep as ocean floors –
all affirm unending love.
Source and strength of every life,
God's love shelters great and small,
satisfies the fiercest thirst,
spreads a feast for one and all.

Save me from the arrogant
and the schemes they perpetrate;
save me from the heavy price
of the sin that shapes their fate;
righteous God, may holiness
be the measure of my days;
and may all my life be spent
under love's eternal gaze.

Metre: **77 77 D**
Aberystwyth

The righteous have a lifelong aim:
to make the Lord their chief delight,
to hold his word within their hearts,
to speak and stand for what is right.
He bids us turn our thoughts away
from anger and anxiety,
to walk the path of patient trust
and eager generosity.

The righteous have a heritage:
yet not in things that they possess,
and not in wielding earthly power,
but in the God of faithfulness:
his word restores us if we fall;
his care supplies our every need;
he brings us safely through our trials –
in him we are secure indeed.

The righteous have a destiny:
a future home, a promised land,
a hope to cherish in the times
when evil forces are at hand.
With all their self-defeating threats
such powers will soon be swept away;
then shall the saints enjoy God's peace,
fulfilled in his eternal day.

Metre: **88 88 D (DLM)**
Jane (David Peacock)

Inclusive language variations
1.3   to gather wisdom in their hearts
1.5   So let us turn our thoughts away
2.4-8   but in the God of faithfulness
        whose word restores us if we fall,
        whose care supplies our every need,
        who brings us safely through our trials –
        in whom we are secure indeed.
3.8   fulfilled in God's eternal day.

38   The weight of guilt

Lord, I ask you to be gentle,
not to cause me undue strain,
for your hand lies heavy on me
and your arrows bring me pain!
How the weight of guilt I bear
drives me headlong to despair!

When the friends whom I have trusted
seem to turn on me with scorn,
when my heart is crushed with numbness
until all day long I mourn,
grief is mine no words can tell,
anguish I cannot dispel.

So afraid my feet are slipping,
all to you I now confess:
is my own sin not a factor
in the roots of my distress?
Saviour, mercy! Hear me cry –
Lord, I wait for your reply.

Metre: **87 87 77**
Latvia; All Saints

Lord, show me how to count my days,
for life is like a single breath:
so swift, the passing of the years,
so brief, the course from birth to death;
and all my labour seems in vain,
however great the wealth I gain.

I have no hope, except in you,
so show me mercy for my sin;
nor let my heart be overwhelmed
as I receive your discipline.
In hushed and holy awe I stand:
I feel my pain; I sense your hand.

But why should those who scorn your name
derive enjoyment from my fear?
I keep my feelings to myself
whenever godless ears are near;
yet how the fires within me burn
until, at last, to you I turn.

A stranger in the midst of life,
a rootless traveller passing through,
I ask you, Lord, to hear my prayer,
and not to spurn my cry to you;
but let me find, instead of tears,
sufficient joys for all my years.

Metre: **88 88 88**
Melita

Out of life's quagmire I was rescued –
this is my song, my tale to tell:
hearing how you, Lord, answered my prayer,
others will honour you as well.
    Blessed are those who choose to trust you,
    leaving all other gods behind;
    unnumbered miracles of mercy
    such folk are privileged to find.

Should I rely on ritual offerings?
Would they be all that you require?
Have you not written life's instructions?
Your will, my God, is my desire!
    You see my willingness to witness –
    how could I hide your word away?
    Love must be central to my lifestyle,
    truth at the heart of all I say.

Yet, Lord, again I cry for mercy:
may truth and love enfold my life –
more sins are mine than I can number;
my days are seldom free of strife:
    come quickly, Lord – my foes pursue me;
    show them how sin will bring them shame.
    You are my rescuer and helper –
    with all your saints I praise your name.

Metre: **98 98 D**
Rendez à Dieu; Hatfield (Timothy Blinko)

In full integrity

Teach me, Lord, your compassion
for those worn down by strain:
by raging conflicts all around,
by searing inner pain;
for I will need your comfort
when trouble reaches me –
when pressure and ill-health expose
how fragile life can be.

May I avoid the outlook
which always thinks of blame,
of seeing others' sufferings
as proof of guilty shame;
nor let me be the reason
for friendships torn in two –
no slander spread, no trust abused,
in what I say and do.

For times when I have failed you
I ask your mercy, Lord;
for grace to lead a fruitful life,
and peace in you restored;
so let me walk before you
in full integrity,
to worship you throughout my days
and all eternity.

Metre: **76 86 D**
St Margaret; Millie (Norman Warren)

42 & 43 My soul, this sorrow

My God, I long to meet you;
I thirst, as in a drought;
my joy is drained by sceptics
intent on sowing doubt.
With sadness I remember
those days of eager song,
how once I led the worship
among the festive throng:

Then why, my soul, this sorrow?
Must anguish cloud my days?
My hope is in my Saviour –
yes, he shall have my praise!

To lofty mountain ridges,
or under crashing waves –
no matter where life takes me,
I trust the One who saves.
Though pain afflicts my body,
though taunting foes abound,
though sometimes God seems absent,
his love is all around:

Defend me, God, in conflict,
and make my cause your own:
with you to be my stronghold,
why should I mourn and groan?
Illuminate my pathway
and teach me what is right;
to live with you is freedom,
to worship you, delight:

Metre: **76 76 Triple**
Thaxted

Inclusive language variations
R.4   *my God shall have my praise!*
2.7-8 though sometimes you seem absent,
       your love is all around:

Such tales are heard from long ago
of all that you have done;
by your hand, not by mortal skill,
were all those victories won.
    Our triumphs still depend on you –
    how little human strength can do! –
Lord, you shall be our lifelong hope,
    our praise the whole day through.

But now like people sold as slaves
we languish in disgrace;
a fearful, scattered flock we are,
with hungry wolves to face.
    Now plundered, humbled, put to flight,
    we feel abandoned in the fight:
why must we face our neighbours' taunts,
    their words of scorn and spite?

We know you see the secret thoughts
of hearts that go astray,
yet we have kept your covenant,
and not turned from your way;
    but if these trials are ours to share
    for your sake, Lord, whose name we bear,
then by your swift assistance prove
    your never-failing care.

Metre: **86 86 88 86**
The Staff of Faith

Royal Master

For the honour of our King,
every skill we have, we bring:
no one stirs the heart to sing
    like our royal Master.

When he speaks, the truth is heard,
grace and power in every word:
falsehood trembles at the sword
    of our royal Master.

Righteousness and joy are found,
lasting justice will abound,
all because the King is crowned
    as our royal Master.

See the splendour of the bride
led in honour to his side –
chosen, loved and beautified
    by her royal Master.

Now, and to eternal days,
all God's people join to raise
one unending song of praise
    to our royal Master.

Metre: **77 76**
St Alban (Timothy Blinko)

God is our refuge, God is our strength –
in our distress his presence is near;
so though the earth quake under our feet,
safe is his keeping, what shall we fear?

Constantly with us, faithful and strong –
God is our shield, our hope and our song.
Be still and know that he is the Lord,
ever revered and ever adored!

There is a city founded by God,
filled with his glory, held in his care;
nations may fall and kingdoms collapse –
still it remains, that city we share:

Come, see his works, his marvellous deeds,
bringing to nought the power of the sword.
He is exalted over the earth –
humbly confess that he is the Lord:

Metre: **99 99** refrain **99 99**
Blessed Assurance; Manor Road (Michael Higgins)

47   All the earth, exalt the King

Come from nations far and wide;
bow in awe of God Most High;
clap your hands, extol the Lord;
raise a shout, a joyful cry:
thank him for the honoured place
kept for all the heirs of grace.

Hear the festal trumpet-blast;
join the great triumphal roar;
make the swelling tide of song
louder, longer than before.
All the earth, exalt the King:
praise him with the psalms you sing.

Rulers of the world, draw near:
you belong to him alone.
Bring your homage now to God,
to the One on heaven's throne:
hail the everlasting Lord –
come, acclaim, rejoice, applaud!

Metre: **77 77 77**
England's Lane

The Lord who reigns in Zion
has made his glory known:
how splendid is the city
he chose to be his own,
for there he has established
his presence and his throne.

When Zion faced an onslaught
of fierce hostility,
her enemies were routed
and swiftly forced to flee –
the God who lives within her
is her security.

There, in God's holy temple,
his love compels our gaze;
his righteousness inspires us
to fill the world with praise,
until our friends and neighbours
are drawn to seek his ways.

And every generation
can learn from those before,
yet find in Zion's beauty
new riches to explore:
our God is with his people,
both now and evermore!

Metre: **76 76 76**
Paddington (David Terry)

Beyond this age

Come, one and all, from near and far,
to share the insights I have found:
a heart which has been taught by faith
informs the wisdom I expound.

Some flaunt their gold, some trust its power –
but what they cherish will decay;
and still the ransom for a soul
remains a price too great to pay.

Though wealth or learning may be ours,
or fame that spreads throughout the land,
the shackles of mortality
prevent so much that we have planned.

Beyond this age of shame and sham
we glimpse a better destiny:
the Lord will lift us free from death
to walk with him eternally.

Why crave renown or opulence?
They fade, those things we now possess;
our hope, our life are in the Lord,
the God we honour and confess.

Metre: **88 88 (LM)**
Bow Brickhill

The mighty God addresses all creation:
in storm and flame he speaks from heaven's throne.
From east to west the word of summons echoes
to gather those he called to be his own;
and though his righteousness pervades the cosmos,
the judge himself now makes his judgements known.

He has no need of sacrificial rituals –
of lavish gifts, or offerings made by fire;
he holds the earth, with all its teeming creatures –
each one is his; what more could he require?
But thankful hearts, and vows which are
   remembered,
and humble prayers fulfil the Lord's desire.

Yet who would dare bring empty words of homage
and disregard the challenge to obey?
If we indulge our passion, greed or slander,
does he not grieve to see us go astray?
With thankful hearts, and open to your voice, Lord,
we come to seek your new and living way.

Metre: **11 10 11 10 11 10**
Finlandia; Eucalyptus (Rosalie Bonighton)

Have mercy on me, loving Lord,
for I have sinned so much:
in your compassion let me feel
your gracious, cleansing touch.

My many sins I know too well;
I find your verdict true:
throughout my life my inmost thoughts
have seldom honoured you.

Create in me a willingness
to leave those things behind –
and may the joy your Spirit brings
sustain my heart and mind.

Then I shall tell my neighbours, too,
where mercy can be found,
till others turn to you in faith,
and hymns of praise resound.

For contrite hearts are your delight –
what more do you require?
The offerings born of brokenness
are all that you desire.

Metre: **86 86 (CM)**
St Fulbert; St Gilbert (Elizabeth Hill)

I flourish in your presence, Lord –
I thrive on meeting you! –
and with your saints I celebrate
your mercies, old and new:
your love surrounds me all my days:
for ever I will sing your praise.

Though godless schemers flaunt their sin
with every boastful word,
though in their sharp and shameful talk
deceitful plans are heard,
your love surrounds me all my days:
for ever I will sing your praise.

Should 1 pursue prosperity
at someone else's cost?
What profit is eternal shame,
both life and riches lost?
Your love surrounds me all my days:
for ever I will sing your praise.

I flourish in your presence, Lord –
I thrive on meeting you! –
and with your saints I celebrate
your mercies, old and new:
your love surrounds me all my days:
for ever I will sing your praise.

Metre: **86 86 88**
Steyning (Simon Lesley)

God ever present

Who dares imagine a life spent without you?
How would we know what was wrong, what was
    right?
How could we handle our questions of conscience,
scorning your presence and spurning the light?

All of us sometimes pretend you are absent,
living as if life were merely our own,
slow to discover the wisdom you offer,
lured by the sin that we ought to disown.

Then in our moments of crisis we flounder,
torn by the choice between panic and prayer,
till, in our grateful relief, we acknowledge:
yes, you protect us – for yes, you are there!

Yes, you alone are our wisdom, our comfort;
only in you can our joy be restored.
Yes, we admit it – we need you to help us,
God ever present, our Saviour, our Lord.

Metre: **11 10 11 10**
Epiphany Hymn; Tegner (Betty Roe)

Still I am protected

God of might, I call to you:
show me your salvation!
In your name I put my trust,
my hope of vindication.

Ruthless strangers hunt me down;
evil foes assail me;
still I am protected, Lord,
for you will never fail me.

When you undermine such threats,
when such dreams are blighted,
your deliverance renders me
both grateful and delighted.

Metre: **76 77**
Puer Nobis

Morning, noon and night I plead

Morning, noon and night I plead:
terror grips my heart and mind;
    those who taunt me, those who stare,
    push me closer to despair.
How I yearn to fly away,
leaving trouble far behind.

Where am I to turn for help?
In our cities, lies are rife;
    there abuse and malice lurk,
    there destruction is at work.
Lord, dispel those deadly threats;
stem the violence, end the strife.

Yet a deeper wound is mine:
cold betrayal by a friend –
    treacherous and insincere,
    someone whom I once held dear;
then, we worshipped side by side;
now, my anguish knows no end.

Lord, will justice not prevail?
Will you let the righteous fall?
    Will your mercy not sustain
    those who cry to you in pain?
Saviour God, in you I trust;
and in faith to you I call.

Metre: **77 77 77**
Heathlands

I entrust myself to you 56

Mercy, God! My foes pursue me:
swift and savage, their attack,
fuelled by pride and filled with slander,
chasing, never holding back.
All day long they plot to harm me,
blithely twisting what I say,
lurking in the shadows, spying,
keen to snatch my life away:

Human foes may rage against me –
in the end, what can they do?
Your word quells my rising panic;
I entrust myself to you.

Lord, you heard my call for justice;
you have counted all my tears;
once again I sense your mercy
as the onslaught disappears!
I remain a grateful debtor,
freed from death to sing your praise;
saved from danger, I will serve you,
walk with you through all my days:

Metre: **87 87 D** refrain **87 87**
Runciman

Be gracious to me, Saviour God,
the haven where I hide;
protect me till the trauma fades,
till storm and flood subside.
I call to you, the Lord Most High,
whose love is sure to last:
your word rebukes the angry mob;
your purpose holds me fast.

God, may your splendour dwarf the heavens
and fill the world with light
when I encounter fearsome beasts
who brandish words of spite;
but whether it is pits they dig,
or nets to snare my feet,
if your hand makes their schemes rebound,
their rout will be complete.

Lord, I intend to wake the dawn
with songs for you to hear,
and I will sing your faithfulness
to nations far and near:
your love is broader than the skies,
beyond the highest height:
God, may your glory dwarf the heavens
and set the world alight!

Metre: **86 86 D (DCM)**
Vox Dilecti

For justice

Will our rulers stand for justice,
or will evil win the day?
Might they prove unworthy leaders,
bent on falsehood, come what may?
    Words of venom,
      deeds of violence –
is it these they will pursue?
Have they nothing else in view?

Lord, restrain vindictive rulers,
all whose aims conflict with yours:
limit their ferocious scheming;
halt the harm their threats could cause:
    such abhorrence –
      Lord, abort it!
Drain their power away, we plead;
never let their plans succeed.

Swiftly, Lord, fulfil your kingdom;
make ungodly empires fall;
let your people find contentment
knowing you are Lord of all.
    In your mercy,
      in your goodness,
in your judgements we delight,
God, forever just and right.

Metre: **87 87 44 77**
Cwm Rhondda

59   Like dogs

God, save me from this onslaught,
my foes' hostility,
for nothing in my conduct
deserves their savagery.
Like dogs they snarl in anger,
with threats in every word;
to you they pose no problem,
my strength, my loving Lord.

Protect me from their cursing;
declare their words untrue;
yet teach me through this crisis
to place my trust in you;
and by your intervention,
Lord, make it clearly known
that you, the God of Jacob,
still reign from heaven's throne.

Like dogs, they growl with hunger
and search for prey to kill;
they find no satisfaction
and never have their fill;
but you, Lord, are my refuge,
your love, tomorrow's song;
through all my times of trouble,
in you I am made strong.

Metre: **76 76 D**
Aurelia

The timeless certainties of love

When times of desperation come
and all creation seems to shake,
when people stagger drunkenly
for fear the very earth might break,
amid estrangement from the Lord
the heart cries out for hope restored.

But is there not a flag unfurled,
a banner raised against the foe,
a refuge and a place of help
where those who fear the Lord can go?
God's saving power will surely prove
the timeless certainties of love.

For still, across the centuries,
the ancient words of promise stand:
in triumph and in holiness
God owns and governs every land;
each land, each person he will use
as he and he alone shall choose.

Our hope is in your mercy, Lord:
mere human strength cannot succeed.
If you disown us, we must fail;
will you not grant the help we need?
Through conflict or calamity,
you are our only victory.

Metre: **88 88 88**
Melita

61 My focus all my days

Lord, listen to my cry,
this faint yet urgent plea,
and guide me homeward to a place
of real security.

My Refuge and my Tower
from foes on every side,
the shelter you alone can give
is where I long to hide.

You know that all my vows
were made for you to hear;
the heritage you gave to me
is built on godly fear.

Protect your servant's life
within your timeless care,
and may your perfect love become
the crown and shield I bear.

For then my heart's delight
shall be to sing your praise:
my pledge to honour you will be
my focus all my days.

Metre: **66 86 (SM)**
Sandys; Grosmont (Robert Jones)

Be my Refuge

God my Refuge and my Rest,
God my Fortress, firm and sure,
God my Saviour and my Hope,
in your strength I stand secure.

When my foes devise their schemes,
when they mouth their cunning lies,
you discern their true intent –
who can take you by surprise?

Frail indeed is human strength,
yielding scant security;
brief indeed are earthly lives,
measured by eternity.

Though my riches multiply,
I will trust in you, my Lord:
may my heart be yours alone,
and your favour, my reward.

Be my Refuge and my Rest;
be my Fortress, firm and sure;
be my Saviour and my Hope,
God in whom I stand secure.

Metre: **77 77**
Emma; Fontenay (Richard Lloyd)

63 My trust and triumph

Within my heart a desert lies –
an empty land, a barren place –
and like a traveller racked with thirst
I long for you, the God of grace.

Your power and glory once I knew:
those memories still enthral my mind –
they tell me that your presence brings
a feast for hungry souls to find.

When anxious thoughts disrupt my sleep,
to your unfailing care I cling
till, lifted by your tender strength,
my weary spirit starts to sing.

Whatever troubles lie ahead,
your constant love will see me through:
my God, my joy, I sing your praise –
my trust and triumph are in you.

Metre: **88 88 (LM)**
*Church Triumphant; O Righteous Lord;
Upnor (Norman Warren); St Peter;
Hall Green (Andrew Fletcher)*

Save me from my enemies

Listen, Lord, to my complaint –
save me from my enemies,
from the noisy, wicked mob
with their vile conspiracies.

From their practised, poisoned tongues
brash and bitter words I hear:
words to snare the innocent,
threats without a trace of fear.

How they spur each other on
in their cruel and cunning schemes –
to devise the perfect crime
is the focus of their dreams.

Lord, you hear their boastful speech –
cause their evil plots to fail;
make them understand at last
what distress their plans entail.

Then shall people far and near
pause and contemplate your ways –
then your servants will rejoice,
trust in you and sing your praise.

Metre: **77 77**
Ephraim; Zachary (Norman Warren)

65   How lavishly you give

We owe our thanks to you, Lord –
how lavishly you give!
And how we love your presence –
where better could we live?
Yet all our finest worship
can never clear our debt
for prayers that you remember,
for sins that you forget.

Your might is awe-inspiring,
too vast for words to tell:
what lofty peaks you fashion,
what surging seas you quell!
Your word commands the nations
to spurn their evil ways,
till those who see your wonders
respond with reverent praise.

For nature's steady rhythms
with all that they provide,
for each abundant harvest
and tables well-supplied,
we join the thankful chorus
of forest, hill and field
to honour you, the Giver,
for all creation's yield.

Metre: **76 76 D**
Ellacombe

Let all the earth bring joyful songs to God
   to praise his name,
whose awe-inspiring deeds and matchless power
   extend his fame.

He drove the sea apart for Israel's sake,
   and led them free –
for yes, the Lord sees every human trial
   and tragedy.

Through troubled times the Lord has held us safe
   and made us strong;
let all whose lives have prospered in his love
   take up the song.

And those to whom the faithfulness of God
   has been revealed:
may heartfelt worship be the sacrifice
   they choose to yield.

For by the inmost longings of our hearts
   God weighs our prayer –
so let us sing with reverent gratitude
   for all his care.

Metre: **10 4 10 4**
Tribe Road (Colin Mawby)

The kindness of his face

May God be gracious, granting us his favour,
shining on us the kindness of his face,
so that his sovereign purpose of salvation
may stand revealed to all the human race.

May all the peoples lift their hearts in worship;
may every nation bring its joyful song;
may they exalt the God who guides and judges,
upholding right and overturning wrong.

Then shall the earth rejoice in God's abundance –
more than enough for every nation's need!
When all the peoples honour his intentions,
then shall we know God's gracious touch indeed.

Metre: **11 10 11 10**
Lord of the Years; Welbourn (John Marsh)

Inclusive language variations
1:1-3   May God be gracious, granting us great
       favour,
      shining on us a kind and loving face,
      so that the sovereign purpose of salvation
3:3   When all the peoples honour right intentions

May God, our God, arise

May God, our God, arise,
put all his foes to flight,
and show his saving power
in majesty and might:
though battles rage, come good or ill,
we know God's love enfolds us still.

The Lord upholds the weak
and calls the lonely friends;
unshackled hearts enjoy
the freedom he extends:
our burdens every day he bears –
he sees, he understands, he cares.

The food our bodies need
his gracious hand supplies,
and with abundant gifts
he takes us by surprise –
but more than this: he feeds the soul;
his word makes broken spirits whole.

Enveloped in such love,
we worship and rejoice:
we glorify the Lord
with instrument and voice;
let every nation join the song –
the Lord is faithful, just and strong.

Yes, let the nations come,
their finest gifts to bring,
and bow in reverent fear
before the sovereign King;
let all who share his victory
proclaim his awesome majesty!

Metre: **66 66 88**
Darwall's 148th

Peace in your promise

Rescue me, God: the floods engulf me;
deep is the hatred I am shown;
see what demands are placed upon me;
guilt, too, which I cannot disown.
Though I am treated as an outcast,
deluged with insults in your name,
Lord, keep my hope in you unshaken,
nor let me bring your people shame.

Sharp are the arrows of derision,
bitter, the flavours of disgrace;
come quickly, Lord, as my deliverer;
show me the kindness in your face.
All who indulge in persecution,
must they not answer for their ways?
Will they not forfeit life's best treasures,
those who have spurned you all their days?

From my distress I cry in worship,
raising a song of thanks to you;
let all who hear it be encouraged,
knowing your care enfolds them, too.
So let the whole creation praise you,
Lord, for your people's hope is sure:
peace in your promise of salvation,
home in your presence evermore.

Metre: **98 98 D**
Rendez à Dieu

Helper and Deliverer

In the day of looming trouble,
    Lord, rescue me;
God my Helper and Deliverer,
    answer my plea.
Danger heightens my awareness
of my poverty and weakness –
I depend on your salvation:
    swift may it be!

Those who come with plans to harm me –
    turn them away;
and on all who plot my downfall,
    send disarray.
Even some who walk beside me
taunt me, threaten or deride me:
let their shameful schemes be thwarted;
    keep them at bay.

Lord, may all who love your mercy
    sing day and night,
knowing that the highest honours
    are yours by right:
for, though countless trials assail us,
we know you will never fail us,
God our Helper and Deliverer,
    God our Delight.

Metre: **84 84 88 84**
Ar Hyd Y Nos

All day long

God, my ever-present refuge
from the harm my foes intend,
hear my call for your protection:
on your answer I depend.
    Many tongues predict my downfall –
    I trust you to make me strong:
    God, my Rock, my hope since childhood,
    I will praise you all day long.

Though my earthly years are passing,
though my life may soon be gone,
let tomorrow's generation
hear me tell what you have done.
    When accusers stand against me,
    when they scheme to do me wrong,
    confident in you, my Saviour,
    I will praise you all day long.

Righteous God, the God of wonders,
who can be compared to you?
Though I suffer countless troubles,
you are sure to bring me through.
    Holy God, forever faithful,
    your deliverance is my song:
    by your mercy saved and shielded,
    I will praise you all day long.

Metre: **87 87 D**
Austria; Milan (Colin Mawby)

Let the King be crowned

God has given us a King:
how good his reign will be,
for the realm which he commands
will last eternally;
    and with justice he will speak
    to defend the poor and weak –
in his holiness we find
our souls' prosperity.

To the limits of the earth
the Victor's reign extends,
and the tribute shall be his
which every nation sends.
    With the righteousness of God
    he will break the tyrant's rod,
for the victims of the cruel
he counts as honoured friends.

Let the finest gold be brought,
and let the King be crowned;
through his kingdom, far and wide,
may lasting fruit abound.
    May the blessings from his hand
    cover this and every land,
till the earth is filled with praise,
one vast, unending sound.

Metre: **76 76 77 76**
Kelvingrove; Victor (Andrew Wright)

Good to all his people

God is good to all his people
so with joy we sing and shout:
God is good, without a doubt!

In a world of shady dealing,
    seems the wicked always gain,
    full of pride and free of pain;
it is tempting then to wonder:
    is the calling to be pure
    worth the struggles we endure?

If our anger makes us utter
    things that no one ought to say
    and we start to slip away,
still the Lord is very gracious:
    we can trust him as the friend
    who is faithful to the end:

When we see from his perspective
    we begin to understand
    what the Holy One has planned:
there will come a time for judgement –
    those who build on shaky ground
    in the end will not be found:

Since the Lord is ours for ever,
    what on earth could we require?
    What in heaven could we desire?
And when mortal powers are failing,
    God remains our strength and song,
    for to him our lives belong:

As we follow where he leads us,
    he will guide us all our days
    and instruct us in his ways
till our earthly years are over,
    and we live for evermore
    with the Lord whom we adore:

Metre: **8 77 D** refrain **8 77**
Wootton Bassett

Remember, Lord

Lord God, have you rejected us,
the very people whom you chose?
Are you too angry now to care
how we are treated by our foes?

With unimpeded savagery
they ruined every sacred place:
remember, Lord, the crushing blows
your people were obliged to face.

No wondrous signs now show your might;
we hear no clear, prophetic word –
will you not vindicate your name
where so much blasphemy is heard?

But you are the Creator God
who filled the void with life and light,
who gave the cosmic chaos form
and shaped the flow of day and night.

Remember, Lord, your promises;
remember, Lord, your people's pain;
remember, Lord, your foes' contempt –
and reassert your holy reign!

Metre: **88 88 (LM)**
O Righteous Lord; Memorare (Andrew Moore)

Who else but you

Great God whose presence we have known,
we bring our thanks to you,
astounded by your sovereign power,
amazed at all you do.

What gain is travelling half the world
for riches or renown,
when you alone exalt the meek
and bring the haughty down?

Who else but you appoints the time
for judgement to begin,
or pours the cup of bitterness,
the consequence of sin?

Lord, may we never shirk your call
to challenge what is wrong –
and may the praise of Jacob's God
for ever be our song.

Metre: **86 86 (CM)**
University; Market Street (Andrew Fletcher)

Great is the Lord, renowned among his people;
where they assemble, he is surely there:
this is our God, the shield to every arrow;
this is our God, the lion in his lair.

He is majestic, more than ancient mountains;
he is resplendent, robed in dazzling light;
at his rebuke the tools of war lie broken,
the valiant warriors sleep in endless night.

God will arise, the judge of all the peoples,
and in that day of justice, who shall stand?
He will pronounce his verdict on oppression
and save the meek, his saints in every land.

Even the fiercest raging heart will praise him
when, bearing gifts, the nations bow in fear –
when mortal pride is stilled in silent homage
before the Lord whom heaven and earth revere.

Metre: **11 10 11 10**
Highwood; Intercessor

Unseen footsteps

From my aching inner turmoil,
from my night of deep distress,
from the musings and the memories
of a soul so comfortless
came my cries for you to help me –
groans that words could not express.

Bygone years and songs once cherished:
these it was I thought about;
still the fear of your rejection
raised an element of doubt:
'Has the Lord forgotten mercy?
Has unfailing love run out?'

Yet when I considered history,
countless ages told anew
of your many striking wonders –
power revealed in all you do!
Jacob's God, and Joseph's Saviour,
who is holy, Lord, like you?

How the oceans writhed before you!
Lightning flashed at your command!
Driving back the sea, you planted
unseen footsteps on the land;
calling Moses, choosing Aaron,
you led Israel by the hand.

Metre: **87 87 87**
Picardy

The wisdom of the past,
the lessons we have heard,
show God's astounding deeds –
and how our forebears erred;
may we obey the things we learn,
and teach our children in their turn.

A cloud that led the way;
a wind to part the seas;
and water from a rock:
the Lord sent all of these!
Shall we forget God's power to save,
or spurn the law of life he gave?

For Israel's grumbling words
provoked God's angry fire:
so shallow was their faith,
so godless their desire!
He gave them ample quail to eat,
but sent them judgement with that meat.

What fickle, stubborn hearts!
What slowness to repent!
How little they believed
that all God said, he meant!
And yet his mercy still remained:
their sins forgiven, his wrath restrained.

Dare we forget, like them,
the price that has been paid,
the suffering and the blood
that saw atonement made?
And dare we test our God, our rock,
the shepherd who redeemed the flock?

continued

They bowed to other gods,
defiled the promised land,
and disobeyed the Lord
who led them by the hand.
He took his presence far away
and threw their lives in disarray.

But then in sovereign power
he underlined his will:
to build a sanctuary
on Zion's holy hill;
so Israel found, through David's reign,
God's gracious care confirmed again.

Metre: **66 66 88**
St John (Adoration)

Inclusive language variations
2.5-6 Shall we forget such power to save,
        or spurn the law of life God gave?
3.2   provoked such angry fire
3.5   God gave them ample quail to eat,
4.4-6 that all God said was meant!
        And yet such mercy still remained:
        their sins forgiven, God's wrath restrained.
6.4-5   who led them by the hand
        but took the presence far away
7.2   God underlined that will:

How long, Lord

Lord, hear your people's cry:
what hardships they have faced!
The faithful suffer ridicule,
their cities are laid waste;
denied the dignity
of burying their dead,
your servants wonder whether, soon,
their own blood must be shed.

How long, Lord, will it be
until you hear our prayer?
Let those deprived of hope and home
be conscious of your care;
and all whose brutal schemes
provoke such bitter pain –
how long, Lord, till your enemies
acknowledge that you reign?

Renew your people's strength
and spare them further shame;
Lord, make your holy presence known
and vindicate your name!
Let every nation see
the justice of your ways,
till all your servants join to sing
your everlasting praise.

Metre: **66 86 D (DSM)**
Gobaith; Leaghur (June Nixon)

80   Show your face

Shepherd of the chosen flock,
mighty One, enthroned on high,
God whom angel hosts adore,
hear our humble, ardent cry:
let your glory flood our sight!
Rise in holy, saving might:

Show your face in mercy, Lord –
may your people be restored.

How long will your anger blaze?
How long will you spurn our prayer?
How long must our bitter tears
bring a foretaste of despair?
From our neighbours we have borne
cruel contempt and brazen scorn:

Once you cleared a plot of land,
planting there a tender vine;
there it spread its leafy boughs,
there its fruit was lush and fine.
Now that fruit, abandoned, falls;
broken are the vineyard walls:

Recognise our deep distress:
Lord, your vine is now laid waste;
see the saints whom once you chose
now, at your rebuke, disgraced.
Let your call again be known,
claim your servants as your own:

Metre: **77 77 77** refrain **77**
St George's Windsor; Pastor Gregis (Andrew Fletcher)

Sing with every kind of music!
Shout for all the world to hear!
Celebrate unchanging kindness
in a festive atmosphere!
God commands our jubilation;
we have ample grounds for praise –
was not our salvation purposed
long before the dawn of days?

Slaves to sin, ensnared by habit:
who could fathom our distress?
But the Lord's own intervention
summoned us to holiness.
Other powers demand allegiance –
let us heed their call no more:
God who gave us life and freedom
still has countless gifts in store.

Dare we look for God's approval
if we spurn the call to grace?
Could we hope to find assistance
in the many trials we face?
Yet to all who hear and follow
comes a pledge of lasting worth:
sharing both eternal triumph
and the richness of the earth.

Metre: **87 87 D**
Ode to Joy; Abbot's Leigh

The cry goes up

The cry is heard from heaven:
the Judge presides in court!
He questions our integrity
by judgements we distort.

The voiceless, powerless poor
are harassed to despair;
their welfare is God's charge to us;
their cause is ours to share.

But those who rule this world
choose wilful ignorance,
till all creation quakes in shame
before such insolence.

For holy dignity
the human race was made;
but mortal nature, flawed by sin,
leaves hearts and hopes betrayed.

The cry goes up to heaven:
'Lord, make your justice known,
for all the earth is yours to judge,
and every land, your own.'

Metre: **66 86 (SM)**
Carlisle

Inclusive language variations
1.2-3   the Judge presides in court
      and questions our integrity
5.2   God, make your justice known,

Speak, Lord

Speak, Lord, and let us hear again
your potent, living word;
reveal yourself in acts of might
and let your voice be heard.

For evil powers are hard at work:
they cunningly conspire;
your people's downfall, nothing less,
remains their chief desire.

From every side, from deep within,
they threaten to attack;
arise, Lord, as you have before:
turn Satan's armies back.

Ignite the fire of holiness
which your opponents fear;
like chaff before the raging wind,
Lord, make them disappear.

Then those who see what you have done
will surely seek your face,
confessing you the Lord Most High,
the God of truth and grace.

Metre: **86 86 (CM)**
St Anne

In your presence

Lord, I dearly love your presence,
more than words can ever tell;
how I yearn to see the beauty
of the courts in which you dwell.
Even sparrows there find refuge;
there the swallow rears her young;
what a joy to have a home there,
where unending praise is sung.

Happy are the pilgrim people
pressing on to greater things,
finding water in the wasteland,
making it a place of springs;
on they go with mounting vigour
till they stand before your throne;
God of Jacob, guard your servants:
make your lasting kindness known.

In the hearts of all the faithful,
grace and glory are revealed –
lavish gifts you give so freely,
mighty Lord, our Sun and Shield.
Better humble, godly service
than a home where sin holds sway;
better one day in your presence
than a thousand far away.

Metre: **87 87 D**
Bethany; Hope Park (Ian Sharp)

Your favour rested on this land
and brought your people mercy, Lord:
the richness of your grace was seen
in countless broken lives restored –
for holy wrath was held at bay
while sin and guilt were swept away.

But your rebuke now weighs us down:
will you be angry evermore?
Deliver us from all our sin,
revive us as you did before;
in your unfailing love renew
the joy your people find in you.

With ears attentive to your voice
and spirits hushed in reverent fear
we come to seek your saving touch,
the word of peace we need to hear:
as we renounce our foolish past,
Lord, make your glory known at last.

May righteousness and peace unite
and justice yield to tenderness;
may loyal hearts be our response
to heaven's gift of holiness –
Lord, fill our lives and flood our land
with all your gracious love has planned.

Metre: **88 88 88**
Melita; Gloucester Road (David Terry)

86 In troubled times

Lord, hear my prayer and guard my life!
  Such anguish is before me:
I trust in you, the God I love,
  whose grace and joy restore me.

I call to you in troubled times,
  convinced that you will hear me;
compassionate, forgiving God,
  your love is ever near me.

Your greatness is beyond compare,
  and praised in every nation;
the awesome things you do are sung
  in joyful acclamation.

Your love has spared me from the grave –
  what power has death to hold me?
So may I walk in faithfulness
  to all that you have told me.

Lord, make me strong in troubled times,
  lest ruthless foes confound me;
may praise be all that fills my heart,
  and grace, your comfort round me.

Metre: **87 87 Iambic**
St Columba

City of God

Nowhere can rival the city of God,
loveliest, holiest place in his sight:
there as on mountains of splendour it stands;
there are his people, his lasting delight.

Once we were strangers, but now we draw near,
summoned to faith from the ends of the earth;
now in the city of God we belong:
he has declared it the place of our birth.

Now we are citizens, children and heirs;
now in his presence our hearts are at home;
our names are even recorded in heaven –
Lord, with the music of worship, we come!

Metre: **10 10 10 10**
Slane

Prisoner of despair

Day and night I cry to you:
free me from my gnawing fear;
I am anxious, drained of strength,
marked as one whose death is near –
would I praise you from the grave?
Show me, Lord, your power to save.

How the burden of your wrath
leaves my soul in deep dismay!
Why, so often through the years,
have you turned your face away?
As a prisoner of despair,
am I banished from your care?

Even those I called my friends
now consider me unknown;
driven from my family,
I must bear my grief alone.
In the darkness, asking 'Why?'
night and day to you I cry.

Metre: **77 77 77**
Petra; Diurnus Noctu (Martin Setchell)

Love will be our song for ever,
faithful love from ages past:
love enshrined within a promise
made by you and sure to last;
human tongues and angel voices
join in reverence and delight,
praising your unrivalled splendour,
loving Lord, the God of might.

Heaven and earth alike affirm it:
Lord, you are magnificent!
Evil powers and hidden forces
you have rendered impotent.
At your throne of love and justice
we extol you, faithful King:
blessed are those who learn to trust you –
they have ample cause to sing.

Once, when Israel lacked a leader,
David was the man you chose;
an exalted throne you gave him,
and relief from all his foes;
even when your rebel people
scorned your ways and spurned your law,
still your promise shaped the future:
love enduring evermore.

Now, though, we have felt your anger;
now we find disaster near;
shame is ours instead of triumph,
neighbours see our plight, and sneer.
How much longer till you hear us?
Life is short, so swift our days!
Lord, renew the love you promised –
fill your people's hearts with praise.

Metre: **87 87 D**
Lux Eoi; Newcombe (Michael Higgins)

Our hope, our refuge be

From age to age, Lord, you endure:
from long before the earth,
before you made the mountain peaks
or brought this world to birth;
    from everlasting you are God,
    to all eternity:
    for evermore you are our Lord –
    our hope, our refuge be!

We tremble at your holiness,
for we are merely clay;
Almighty God, your awesome power
could sweep our lives away.
    Although we try to hide our sins,
    to you our guilt is clear –
    but by your mercy may we learn
    to live in godly fear.

To you a thousand years are like
a day, an hour gone by,
but we are like the morning grass:
by evening, frail and dry –
    so teach us how to weigh our lives,
    to number all our days,
    and by your timeless wisdom, Lord,
    instruct us in your ways.

With songs of gladness fill our hearts;
let love adorn our years;
and may unending peace assuage
the past, with all its tears.
    To us and to our children show
    your saving majesty:
    from age to age, Lord, prosper us –
    our hope, our refuge be!

Metre: **86 86 D (DCM)**
St Matthew; Sassafras (Rosalie Bonighton);
Wyesham (Robert Jones); Kingsfold

Within the shelter of the Lord,
at home in his unfailing care,
we trust in his eternal strength
to rescue us from every snare:
how safe it is, this hiding-place
beneath his everlasting wings;
how strong a fortress is our God,
the Mighty One, the King of kings.

Though brutal conflicts scar the day,
though nameless perils fill the night,
God's presence calms our troubled minds
and puts our primal fears to flight.
When sin persists and judgement falls
the true security is ours:
protected by the Lord, we stand,
beyond the grasp of evil powers.

He answers every cry for help;
his love is ours till journey's end –
however long our lives may be,
on God's firm promise we depend.
Who knows what dangers we are spared
since angels guard the way we take?
And all who trust and love the Lord
he pledges never to forsake.

Metre: **88 88 D (DLM)**
God's Presence (Andrew Wright);
Before the Throne (Vikki Cook)

How good

How good it is to give you thanks:
we honour you, our mighty King!
Your endless love, your constant care
inspire the praise we gladly bring
    in word and music, day and night:
    to worship you is our delight.

How glad you make us by your deeds!
Your thoughts are deep, beyond compare!
The greatness of your wonders, Lord,
it is our pleasure to declare;
    to those who place their trust in you
    your glory shines through all you do.

How many fail to grasp the truth,
or hear your voice but turn away;
they flourish now, but disregard
the prospect of a judgement day
    when righteousness and mercy meet
    and signal evil's full defeat.

And yet how gracious is your call,
for you address us now as friends
and guide our lives on fruitful paths
until, at length, our journey ends:
    Lord God, how matchless are your ways!
    How right it is to sing your praise!

Metre: **88 88 88**
St Catherine (Tynemouth); Melita

Robed in majesty

Robed in majesty, he reigns,
sovereign from eternity;
praise the Lord, the God of strength,
robed in awesome majesty.

Firm and sure the world will stand:
here the maker's power is shown –
yet, predating even time,
firmer, surer stands his throne.

Surging seas and pounding waves:
mightier is the Lord than these;
mightier than the breakers' roar,
mightier than those surging seas.

Holiness adorns his house;
age on age will hear his law;
praise the Lord, whose reign upholds
holiness for evermore.

Metre: **77 77**
Savannah

Great Judge of all

Lord, do you see the evil in the world?
Look how the weak are crushed, the poor
    oppressed!
Will you ignore the arrogant and proud,
scorning the anguish of the dispossessed?
    You are the one who fashions eye and ear:
    great Judge of all, you surely see and hear!

You discipline the nations of the earth;
in all your dealings you are just and fair.
Those whom you call your people, you sustain,
making them stronger by the griefs they bear.
    Happy are all who learn to understand
    the love revealed by your correcting hand.

Though we have often felt that all was lost
your faithful care has always brought us through;
still when the threat of evil is so real,
strong is our refuge as we trust in you.
    On your unfailing promise we depend:
    your righteous love will triumph in the end!

Metre: **10 10 10 10 10 10**
Song 1; Yorkshire (Stockport)

Come, celebrate with gladness
the Lord, your mighty King:
no other god is like him,
this God whose praise we sing –
for he is the Creator
of sea and sky and land;
the mountains and the valleys
are held within his hand.

Come, bow in adoration;
come, kneel in godly fear
before our holy Sovereign,
the Saviour we revere.
Our God is our Deliverer,
our strong, eternal Rock,
the Maker of his people,
the Shepherd of his flock.

Come, still your hearts to listen
to all he longs to say,
resolved to be attentive,
committed to obey.
Remember those he punished
who put him to the test –
and strive by faith to enter
God's promised, perfect rest.

Metre: **76 76 D**
Morning Light; Waverley (Colin Mawby)

Bring to God your new, best songs,
    all creation;
raise a hymn of gratitude
    for salvation;
far and wide, throughout the world,
    sound his glory;
he has done amazing things –
    tell the story.

Earth and heavens, revere the Lord,
    your creator;
why exalt some other god?
    He is greater!
His are strength and majesty
    never-ending;
ours, the privilege of praise,
    voices blending.

With the finest you possess
    bow before him;
from the fullness of your heart,
    come, adore him.
See, his beauty floods the earth –
    holy splendour!
Yield to him in reverent fear –
    glad surrender!

All that lurks in human hearts
    he discloses;
all that fails the test of truth,
    he opposes.
Let the earth rejoice in hope
    of his kingdom;
skies and oceans, trees and fields,
    join the anthem!

Metre: 74 74 D
Gwalchmai; Inglewood (June Nixon)

Let all the earth rejoice before the Lord,
whose hidden splendours we have scarcely known;
let all the earth be glad that he is just –
on righteousness the King has built his throne.

But who can bear God's burning, holy flame?
Like wax, the mountains melt when he draws near;
his glory fills the heavens and lights the earth –
let all who see respond in reverent fear.

Those other gods our neighbours choose to serve
compared to him are emptiness and shame:
the Lord Most High, exalted over all,
now summons our allegiance to his name.

Lord, teach us all that holiness demands
till light and joy and freedom mark our days,
till all the earth confesses you as King,
and all its people live to bring you praise.

Metre: **10 10 10 10**
West Ashton; Woodlands; Go Forth;
Brookstone (Andrew Fletcher)

Weaving reverence and excitement

Come with newly-written anthems,
craft your finest psalm or song;
praise the God of marvellous mercy,
our deliverer, swift and strong –
    he reveals his holy kindness
    so that all the world may know:
    never once has he forgotten
    what he promised long ago.

Bring your hymns of celebration;
be creative, and rejoice;
blend as one your skilful playing,
thankful heart and cheerful voice.
    Let the wonders of God's greatness
    be your focus as you sing;
    weaving reverence and excitement,
    raise the shout: the Lord is King!

Sing until the whole creation
echoes to the melody,
till the seas and hills and rivers
join the swelling symphony:
    for he comes, and every nation
    shall receive its just reward –
    sing to greet the God of justice,
    righteous Judge and gracious Lord.

Metre: **87 87 D**
Ode to Joy; Bethany; Stibbington (Stanley Vann)

Holy is he!

Let every nation bow in godly fear
before the Lord whom angels all revere;
lift God's name high for all the world to hear –
holy is he!

Sing out his praise, this King of endless might
who shows his people what is just and right,
for righteousness and truth are his delight –
holy is he!

He gave the sacred law which Moses taught;
to him were Aaron's sacrifices brought;
this is the God whose favour Samuel sought –
holy is he!

This is our God, who hears and answers prayer,
who loathes our sin, but clears the guilt we bear;
before his throne, let heaven and earth declare:
holy is he!

Metre: **10 10 10 4**
Engleberg; Nomen Domini (Andrew Moore)

100   Know that the Lord

Come with a song of joy
and raise a mighty cheer:
people of every tribe and tongue,
come, bow in reverent fear.
Know that the Lord is God:
on him all life depends,
and over every human heart
his watchful care extends.

Come with a grateful heart
and fill his courts with song:
honour the name of him to whom
all praise and thanks belong.
Know that the Lord is good,
his faithfulness is sure,
and his unique, unchanging love
for ever will endure.

Metre: **66 86 D (DSM)**
From Strength to Strength; Shirenewton (Robert Jones)

Let me walk with you

Your love will be my song –
Lord, keep me far from wrong,
   and draw me close to you:
let all that you abhor
be banished evermore
   from what I say and do.

The slanderer's deadly flame,
and schemes that merit shame –
   in these I want no part.
From arrogance and lies,
from pride that clouds the eyes,
   my God, protect my heart.

If anyone should try
to make me live a lie,
   consign their plan to fail;
but gladly will I learn
from all who can discern
   what your commands entail.

Lord, I resolve today
in all I do and say
   to stand for what is true:
your love will be my song,
so keep me far from wrong
   and let me walk with you.

Metre: **66 6 D**
Laudes Domini; Haughmond (Alan Viner)

Your sovereign hand

When loneliness and anguish fill my days,
when I am at the limit of my years,
when folk I meet consider me accursed,
when all my food and drink are ash and tears,
    when sleep eludes me, when my bones all burn –
    Lord, do not hide your face: to you I turn.

Unchanging God, renowned through every age,
will you not hear your servant's heartfelt plea?
Show all the world your glorious tenderness;
give those who fear the grave your liberty;
    and generations yet to come to birth
    will see, and sing your praise across the earth.

For you will rule the heavens and earth you made
till you discard them at the end of time;
but, God eternal, spare my life today,
nor let me face oblivion in my prime.
    Grant me, with all your saints, this hope assured:
    a home for ever in your presence, Lord.

Metre: **10 10 10 10 10 10**
Yorkshire (Stockport)

Sing out, my soul, in gratitude
for all the kindness of the Lord:
for sins forgiven and strength revived,
for health and hope restored.
Shout, shout from a heart set free
to enjoy God's vast generosity;
sing, sing of unfailing love,
the crown of all who fear him.

With justice for the victimised
the Lord has made compassion known –
with mercy he rescinds the guilt
of those he calls his own.
High, high as the heavens above
is the reach of God's never-ending love;
far, far are their sins removed
from those who truly fear him.

He shaped our forebears from the clay;
he understands our mortal frame;
no human parent's tenderness
could ever be the same.
Brief, brief is our earthly day,
like a flower, so easily swept away;
long, long will his love remain,
surrounding those who fear him.

Across the breadth of space and time
the Lord's eternal kingdom stands;
let saints and angels heed his voice
and honour his commands.
All, all that the Lord has made,
let his praise be heard, and his power displayed!
Join, join in the song, my soul,
with all whose hearts revere him!

Metre: **88 86 7 10 77**
Greensleeves; Cluny (Richard Lloyd)

All you have created

We worship you, whose splendour dwarfs the
   cosmos,
whose very clothes are robes of dazzling light;
on wind and cloud you ride across the heavens;
your word bids fiery angels soar in flight.

You made the earth, determining its orbit:
primeval chaos fled at your command.
You send the streams from mountain peak to valley,
and yet prevent them flooding all the land.

The waters flow, till plain and pasture flourish;
the forest thrives – there birds may freely nest;
the thirsty creatures drink and find refreshment;
and human hearts with wine and grain are blessed.

You formed the moon to mark the passing seasons;
you gave the sun, whose radiance lights the day;
as each new morning calls us to your service,
the wildlife of the night-time steals away.

Unnumbered marvels emphasise your wisdom:
who knows what mysteries lie beneath the sea?
Yet every mouth relies on your provision:
without your care, how brief our lives would be.

May you rejoice in all you have created,
though just your glance could set the earth ablaze;
may we direct our lives to bring you pleasure,
and praise you with the song of all our days.

Metre: **11 10 11 10**
Intercessor; O Perfect Love

Sing to the Lord with gratitude and wonder;
in song and story tell what he has done:
let all the nations be inspired to seek him,
the Mighty God, the Lord, the Righteous One.
His promise came to Abraham and Isaac,
a land in which their family could live;
his pledge endures a thousand generations,
a covenant whose riches he delights to give.

Across the years, across the miles they journeyed,
both led and shielded by God's loving hand,
until the scourge of famine struck the nations,
and brought destruction to that promised land.
But even then he marked the path before them
when Joseph entered Egypt as a slave –
a man who rose to prominence and power,
distinguished by the godly counsel which he gave.

So Israel made their home awhile in Egypt;
they grew in numbers and prosperity
till Pharaoh's people dreaded subjugation
and changed their welcome into slavery.
Through Moses, God confronted this injustice,
sent plagues of judgement time and time again,
then by one final blow to Egypt's firstborn
he set his people free and broke their every chain.

They left captivity with ample plunder,
and through an empty desert they were led;
beneath a fiery cloud they were protected,
and with the bread of angels they were fed.
Sing praise to God, whose promise never falters,
who thrills the hearts of those he makes his friends;
who so enriches all he brings to freedom
that they may learn to live their days as he intends.

Metre: **11 10 11 10 11 10 11 12**
Danny Boy; Crossways (John Jordan)

Like them

Your endless love, your mighty acts
surpass what words can tell;
Lord, may the joys your people know
be mine to share as well.

Our rebel forebears rarely grasped
your mercy or your might;
we need your mercy, just like them:
we, too, do wrong not right.

The shallow nature of our faith,
our unrestrained desires
and all our grumbling jealousy
provoke your judgement fires.

Before a metal calf they bowed –
an idol in your place! –
until, by Moses' faithful prayer,
you drew them back to grace.

But when they spurned the promised land
you made your anger plain:
they wandered long on desert paths,
and served the baals again.

At Meribah, the waters flowed:
for Moses, what a price!
In Canaan they defiled themselves
by pagan sacrifice.

Yet those whom once you sold in wrath,
in mercy you restored;
may we, like them, be gathered in
to thank and praise you, Lord.

Metre: **86 86 (CM)**
St Magnus

Come with thanks to offer to the Lord;
bring your praises, honouring his name!
    You he redeemed out of every land,
    come with your songs of his mighty hand –
tell of the freedom you now enjoy;
his saving mercy and power proclaim!

You who found yourselves without a home –
in an empty wilderness you strayed! –
    tell of the Lord who became your guide
    when in confusion for help you cried;
now you are walking a different way,
home to the city that God has made.

Those of you who shunned the Lord's commands,
tasting only bitterness and strife:
    though you rebelled and despised his word,
    when you repented your prayer was heard;
sing of the riches he gave you then:
pardon for sin, and eternal life.

You whose lives were battered by the storms,
tossed in turmoil on a raging sea:
    where could you turn in your fear and grief,
    give up your anguish, and find relief?
Come and rejoice in the God whose power
brought you to land and security.

Now you know the favour of the Lord,
his eternal promises you share;
    know that if trouble should visit you
    God will be with you to bring you through:
ponder the ways of your Lord and King –
praise him because of his endless care!

Metre: **99 99 99**
Untitled tune by John Perkins

Never holding back

Lord, I am determined: I shall praise my King;
early in the morning I shall rise and sing;
praise will be my practice everywhere I go,
never holding back what all the world should know.

Every nation's future lies within your hands;
superpowers are subject to divine commands!
In your care the cosmos finds its destiny –
Lord, how overwhelming is your majesty!

You alone can shape us for the task we face,
overcoming evil by the power of grace;
hear the cry for mercy rising to your throne:
lead us, help us, save us – make your presence
   known!

Metre: **11 11 11 11**
Camberwell; Welsh Newton (Robert Jones)

Surely, Lord

God to whom I bow in worship,
God to whom I turn in prayer,
many tongues are ranged against me,
spreading falsehood everywhere.
Those to whom I offered friendship
show me hatred in reply:
surely, Lord, you will defend me;
surely, Lord, you hear my cry.

If opponents rise against me,
bringing lies before a court;
if they plunder my possessions;
if they want my days cut short –
would they have my children orphaned,
hounded from their native land?
Surely, Lord, you feel my anguish;
surely, Lord, you understand.

They have slandered my intentions:
would I harm the weak and poor?
Callous thoughts and spiteful cursing –
when were these the clothes I wore?
Yet they call my sins a millstone,
and my prayer, a hollow plea –
surely, Lord, no condemnation!
Surely, Lord, you stand with me.

In your mercy, heal my weakness
and the wounds that I have borne;
my accusers have maligned me:
bring to silence all their scorn!
Then with all who know your blessing
I will lift my voice in song:
surely, Lord, you are my Saviour;
surely, Lord, you make me strong.

Metre: **87 87 D**
Bethany; Lux Eoi

As Lord of all

Appointed by the Lord
as Lord of all creation,
you reign in majesty
beyond imagination:
    your eager servants wait
    for all that you command;
    your foes must bow before
    the sceptre in your hand.

The calling of a priest
will rest on you for ever,
confirmed by God's own oath,
a bond that none can sever:
    within yourself you bore
    the cost of priceless grace –
    your sacred role transcends
    the breadth of time and space.

You made this world your home
and shared our pain and pleasure;
in tiredness, hunger, thirst
you felt our mortal measure –
    so gracious sympathy
    and holy wrath shall meet
    when, on that final day,
    you take your judgement seat.

Metre: **67 67 66 66**
Gracias; Nun Danket; Royal Sceptre (Andrew Moore)

They will not be forgotten 111

I will stand with God's people and pour out my
    praise;
I delight in the wonders the Lord has made known,
for righteousness echoes through all that he says,
and his deeds have a splendour which mirrors his
    own.

They will not be forgotten, the things he has done,
for as he rules the nations his power is displayed.
In all that he gives us his kindness is seen;
he will always be true to each promise he made.

As the fear of the Lord is where wisdom begins,
let his precepts instruct us, directing our ways.
So awesome he is, and so holy and just:
let eternity ring with the sound of his praise!

Metre: **12 12 11 12**
Stowey

Joy comes to those who have trusted you, Lord, for
    salvation,
those who obey your commands with unfeigned
    adoration.
    This is our prayer:
    make us more fully aware
holiness is our vocation.

Joy comes to those who have brought up their
    children to fear you,
joy to observe how they live by the truth and revere
    you.
    This is our prayer,
    Lord, for those under our care:
may they be constantly near you.

Joy comes to those who find bountiful giving a
    pleasure,
those who see justice and kindness as riches to
    treasure.
    This is our prayer:
    Lord, make us eager to share;
make your compassion our measure.

Joy comes to those who are sure they will not be
    forsaken,
those with no malice that life with its pains might
    awaken.
    This is our prayer:
    when those who scorn you despair,
Lord, let our faith be unshaken.

Metre: **14 14 4 7 8**
Lobe Den Herren

You servants of the Lord,
declare your Master's fame:
today and through eternity
exalt his name.
Throughout the whole wide world
let joyful worship sound;
by day and night, from east to west,
let praise abound.

Let all the nations bow,
acknowledging his reign,
whose glory even heaven's span
cannot contain:
who is there like the Lord,
too great for words to tell?
Yet every detail of our lives
he knows so well.

The needy and the poor,
rejected by their race,
are those for whom our God prepares
an honoured place;
when family and home
transform our lonely days,
we recognise God's loving touch
and sing his praise.

Metre: **66 84 D**
Leoni; St Swithun (Colin Mawby)

What was it but the presence

When Israel left Egyptian days behind –
that foreign tongue, those years of tyranny –
they were the people chosen as God's own,
their promised land, a holy sanctuary.

At their approach the sea was put to flight,
the Jordan river turned and sped away.
What made those rushing waters draw aside,
the hills and mountains skip like lambs at play?

What was it but the presence of the Lord,
who fills the earth at once with joy and fear,
who brought a flowing spring from solid rock –
let trembling seize the world when God draws near!

Metre: **10 10 10 10**
West Ashton

Enthroned in heaven

The honour, Lord, is yours:
to you all praise be given,
great God of love and faithfulness,
enthroned in heaven.
Though many, far and wide,
are unaware of you,
your sovereign will is evident
in all you do.

Unseen, yet seeing all,
you hear and act and feel,
unlike the shallow fantasies
which some think real –
those idols lack the power
to think or move or speak;
the aid of such unworthy gods
we will not seek.

To all who search for joy,
the pathway is the same:
a call to serve you day by day
and bear your name.
Our ever-faithful Lord,
our Helper and our Shield,
the dreams and fears that shape our lives
to you we yield.

May you, the God of heaven
who set the stars in space,
grant us and all our families
the joys of grace;
may we who live on earth
extol you all our days,
and seize each opportunity
to sing your praise.

Metre: **66 84 D**
Leoni; Honour (Martin Setchell)

Out of the grasp of death

I love you, Lord, for you answered me
    when I was close to despair:
I called for help in a time of strife,
when fears of death overwhelmed my life –
    and found that you heard my prayer.

To those who know of your righteousness,
    your gracious promise is clear:
for your compassion is great indeed,
and your assurance is all I need
    to deal with my anxious fear.

Lord, you delivered my soul from death,
    my life from stumbling and tears;
though few acknowledge your ways are true,
my pledge remains: I shall walk with you
    the rest of my earthly years.

For all the love you have shown to me
    my heartfelt thanks I will bring:
I stand, a debtor to boundless grace
as with your people I take my place,
    confessing you Lord and King.

How great the freedom your service gives –
    no better life could there be! –
till in the hour of my final breath
you lead me out of the grasp of death
    to serve you eternally.

Metre: **97 99 7**
Aigburth Vale; Deben (Betty Roe)

Come, praise the Lord, all you nations:
come, praise the Lord, come to worship and adore
and exalt his name – he is worthy
    to be praised,
    to be praised,
to be praised for evermore.

Come, meet the Lord, all you peoples:
come and rejoice, for his love for you is great
and his faithfulness is unending –
    bless the Lord,
    bless the Lord,
bless the Lord, and celebrate!

Metre: **8 11 9 33 7**
Tarnagulla (June Nixon)

118 Unfailing love

Unfailing love! The Lord our God is good –
let all his chosen people join the song;
    unfailing love has drawn us to his care;
    to him our reverent, thankful hearts belong.

Better to trust God's ever-present help
than human pride or ingenuity;
    better to trust the One who hears our prayer
    and changes anguish into liberty.

So many foes, and threats on every side;
so real, the dangers posed by hostile powers:
    so many foes – and yet, when all seemed lost,
    God's mercy meant the victory song was ours.

The hand of God has made his glory known;
rejoice: what he has done is marvellous!
    The hand of God has touched our inmost hearts
    to teach the disciplines of holiness.

This is the day God's purpose stands revealed:
he builds his kingdom in surprising ways;
    this is the day to come into his courts,
    to kneel in gratitude and shout in praise.

You are our God, our Saviour and our King;
how blessed to be the heralds whom you send!
    You are our God, exalted and adored –
    on your unfailing love our lives depend.

Metre: **10 10 10 10**
Woodlands; St Stephen (David Terry)

Here is the lamp 119a

Here is the route laid out for us to follow:
your word reveals the path we ought to tread.
You teach us how to walk and run in freedom
when by the truth we let ourselves be led –
    so now we pledge to turn our backs on falsehood,
    and to be guided by your law instead.

Here is the spring which offers real refreshment
to weary hearts, worn down by endless strain:
within your word we find such inspiration,
and ample strength to bear our deepest pain.
    Lord, in our lives renew your gracious promise
    and speak the word which makes us strong again.

Here is the lamp by whose illumination
your holy ways lie open to our sight;
here are the keys of knowledge and discernment:
through your commands you show us what is right;
    so, Lord, behind the searching beam of Scripture
    we look for you, the source of perfect light.

Based on selected themes from Psalm 119
Metre: **11 10 11 10 11 10**
Finlandia; Thorpe (Betty Roe)

119b   Your gracious judgements

I delight in your decrees, Lord,
everything you say;
gladly will I hear and follow –
never let me stray.
As I ponder your commandments,
guide me in your living way.

All my hope is in your promise,
firm through ages long;
when I suffer, needing comfort,
your word makes me strong.
Those who spurn the truth may taunt me –
still your precepts are my song.

Founded by your timeless statutes,
earth and heavens endure;
by those selfsame laws you saved me,
making me secure:
how I love your gracious judgements!
I will serve you evermore!

Based on Psalm 119:9-16, 49-56, 89-96
Metre: **85 85 87**
Angel Voices

To stand for truth

You know the pressures I endure;
you see the load I bear;
in my distress I call to you,
the God who answers prayer.

Surrounding me, both near and far,
are those who trade in lies:
the brash rebuttal of the truth,
the subtle compromise.

When anger leads to arrogance
they spurn my calls for peace:
although I argue for restraint,
the threats of war increase.

Yet each unfaithful tongue will quake
before your sharpened sword;
so give me grace, till life is done,
to stand for truth, my Lord.

Metre: **86 86 (CM)**
Shepherd Boy's Song

No peril we encounter

However great the treasures life affords
in status or prosperity,
their transitory nature stands exposed:
they offer scant security.

We trust the Lord whose all-creating word
gave rise to wonders still unknown –
who holds unnumbered stars within his hand
yet loves to make our hearts his own.

Although we may be faced with many trials
and dangers often close at hand,
no peril we encounter has the power
to undermine what God has planned.

And so, in spite of all the grievous wounds
which mar a world whose pain we share,
we sense the details of our daily lives
are held within God's watchful care.

Metre: **10 8 10 8**
River Gums (Rosalie Bonighton)

Inclusive language variations
2.1 We trust the One whose strong, creative word
2.3 the God who holds unnumbered galaxies
2.4 but yearns, our inmost hearts to own.

Jerusalem!

How glad I was to meet my friends
and hear the call to go with them;
how glad to journey till my feet
had reached your gates, Jerusalem.

The company assembling here
is rich in its diversity,
but gathers at the Lord's command,
one body, knit in unity.

Jerusalem! May peace be yours
in every home and citadel;
may justice make your walls secure,
and in your courts may all be well.

Jerusalem! In you I find
my sisters, brothers, treasured friends:
for their sake, may God's wealth be yours,
and such a peace as never ends.

Metre: **88 88 (LM)**
O Waly, Waly

We turn our eyes

We turn our eyes to you,
the Lord on heaven's high throne,
and ask that you, the God we serve,
will make your kindness known.

A watchful servant waits
for every new command;
so we have set our eyes to mark
the moving of your hand.

Will you not heal the scars
of all that we have borne,
the chill contempt of arrogance,
the searing darts of scorn?

We turn our eyes to you,
the Lord on heaven's high throne,
and ask that you, the God we serve,
will make your kindness known.

Metre: **66 86 (SM)**
Franconia

Inclusive language variations
1.2   the One on heaven's high throne,
4.2   the One on heaven's high throne,

Unless the Lord had stood with us –
let all God's people say –
would not the angry storms we faced
have swept our lives away?

Had not the Lord defended us
from such a fierce attack,
who could have met those dreadful foes
and held the onslaught back?

But God, our God, has rescued us
from their brutality:
the fowler's snare is broken now,
the captive birds fly free.

The Maker of the galaxies,
the Lord of earth and heaven,
has promised all the help we need –
all praise to God be given!

Metre: **86 86 (CM)**
St Stephen (Newington); Nisi Dominus (Alan Rees)

Unshakeable for evermore

So firm and sure, those ancient hills
which stand around Jerusalem –
thus all whose faith is in the Lord
will know his power enfolding them:
these are the saints he makes secure,
unshakeable for evermore.

The Lord, the God of holiness,
restrains the rulers of the lands,
to stay the lure of evil deeds
from snaring godly hearts and hands:
corrupt regimes will not remain
to thwart the justice of God's reign.

Lord, honour all whose hearts are pure,
who choose to serve you faithfully,
but undermine the crooked schemes
of those who foster treachery:
cause tyrannies and threats to cease,
and grant your people lasting peace.

Metre: **88 88 88**
Melita; Chactonbury Down (Simon Lesley)

Dream come true

When you brought the captives home
it was a dream come true;
joy and laughter overflowed
in gratitude to you.

For in that call to freedom
a new life had begun,
and even non-believers
confessed what you had done!

All that you have done for us
has filled us with delight;
we have felt your tenderness
and seen your saving might.

But now our souls are barren,
our hearts are desert-dry;
renew us, Lord, revive us –
for streams of grace we cry.

When your servants go in tears
to sow their precious grain,
grant a joyful harvest-hymn
to lead them home again.

Metre: **76 76**
All Things Bright and Beautiful; Royal Oak;
Freedom (John Marsh)

But a house

Can a house be built to last
    unless the Lord is there?
Can a city stand secure
    without his watchful care?
Should our labours never cease,
making earthly wealth increase?
We could miss the gift of peace
    he longs for us to share.

But a house the Lord has built
    could be a dynasty
with an influence for good
    across society.
Lord, the children whom we raise –
may they serve you all their days,
bringing you delight and praise
    throughout eternity.

Metre: **76 76 77 76**
Kelvingrove

Inclusive language variations
1.4 without our Saviour's care?
1.8 which we were meant to share.

The whole of life

Whoever fears the Lord
and lives as he intends
will find the whole of life
is filled with gifts he sends.

When work is more than toil
and reaps a just reward,
when strength and health are ours,
all these are from the Lord!

We celebrate the joys
of home and family,
where love's enduring bonds
provide security.

God nurtures every child
for life's demanding race;
each day he offers us
new fruitfulness, new grace.

His kindness is revealed
where bitter conflicts cease;
far more, within our hearts,
his mercy brings us peace.

May God prolong our days
to see our children's heirs,
and may his gracious gifts
be ours and also theirs.

Metre: **66 66**
Ibstone

Song of triumph

I will sing a song of triumph,
sing to reassert the truth,
sing although unnumbered troubles
have beset me since my youth:
when the conflicts I encountered
left me wounded, scarred and sore,
God the Righteous One was with me
to destroy the chains I bore.

Those who hate what God has chosen:
in the end, how can they thrive?
Plants with neither earth nor moisture,
what can help them to survive?
Those who trust the Lord to save them:
may they find, instead of shame,
kindness from the One they worship,
endless blessings in God's name.

Metre: **87 87 D**
Abbot's Leigh

On your mercy

From the depths my soul cries out:
listen, Lord, to my plea;
on your mercy I depend –
hear my cry and answer me.

If you kept a list of sins
who could stand free of blame?
But forgiveness comes from you –
therefore I revere your name.

More than those who watch at night
for the coming of day –
more than this my eager soul
waits to hear what you will say.

Lord, may those who seek your love
find you faithful and true;
may your endless mercies reach
all who put their hope in you.

Metre: **76 77**
Sutton Manor; Deepdale (Richard Lloyd);
Marton (Andrew Wright)

With such contentment

No lofty dreams are mine,
no cold contempt or pride;
I crave no share in vast concerns
to keep me satisfied.

Within its mother's arms
a child may safely rest;
with such contentment for my soul
I, too, am richly blessed.

In God I am content;
in God I rest secure;
let all his people hope in him,
both now and evermore.

Metre: **66 86 (SM)**
Franconia

Inclusive language variation
3.3   let this be where our hope is fixed

When David had a longing
to build the Lord a house,
he voiced his heart's intention
by means of solemn vows.
His people caught the vision:
to build a sacred place
where holy joy and worship
would please the God of grace.
    Let David be remembered,
    your faithful servant, Lord:
    the depth of his devotion,
    the hardships he endured.

The Lord then vowed to David:
his house would surely last
if only his successors
held God's commandments fast;
God longed to set among them
a throne for heaven's King;
what joy and what abundance
his presence there would bring!
    Let David's Lamp be lighted,
    your chosen Servant, Lord:
    his kingdom be established,
    his triumph be assured.

Metre: **76 76 Triple**
Thaxted

Heartfelt unity

How good it is to share
the heartfelt unity
of brothers knit as one,
of sisters who agree.

For like the sacred oil
on Aaron's head once poured,
the fragrance of shalom
is hallowed by the Lord.

The dew may seem so fresh
on lofty mountain heights –
the love of kindred souls
eclipses such delights.

Where harmony is found,
by God's commanding grace
the vibrant joys of heaven
transfigure time and space!

Metre: **66 66**
Ibstone; Quam Bonum (Alan Rees)

Within the holy place

Bring to the Lord a song of joy,
    for you are called by grace;
lift up your hands in sheer delight
and sacred duty, day and night,
    within the holy place.

So may you meet the Faithful One
    within the holy place;
he who created earth and heaven –
may all his gifts to you be given,
    the riches of his grace.

Metre: **86 88 6**
Gatescarth

Priestly devotion

Come into God's presence to worship and sing,
with glad hallelujahs the offerings you bring;
how good and how pleasant, how fitting it is
to honour the Lord who affirms we are his.

The depths of the oceans, the stars far away –
the whole of creation falls under his sway;
in climates and seasons his power is displayed –
he does as he pleases with all that he made.

When Egypt afflicted the people he chose,
God dealt the oppressor the fiercest of blows;
and kings were dethroned by the Lord's mighty hand
so Israel could enter their long-promised land.

The fame of the Lord will extend evermore –
how unlike the idols some people adore!
Devised by mere mortals, what can they achieve? –
a factor which many decline to perceive.

God's call made you holy, to walk in his sight
in reverent submission and thankful delight –
so come, all God's people, with offerings of praise:
make priestly devotion the crown of your days.

Metre: **11 11 11 11**
St Denio; Priestly Devotion (John Marsh)

Give thanks to God, for he is good:
his greatness, no one else can share;
his love endures for evermore;
his wonders are beyond compare.

His love endures for evermore;
his power and wisdom fashioned space;
his word gave land and ocean form
and set both sun and moon in place.

His love endures for evermore:
his mighty hand, his outstretched arm
freed Israel from their captors' grasp,
confounding those who did them harm.

His love endures for evermore:
he drove a pathway through the sea
and rescued Israel from the threat
of their pursuing enemy.

His love endures for evermore,
affirmed through all he pledged to give;
so he let no one steal the lands
where Jacob's tribes were meant to live.

His care ensures our needs are met
and dignity and hope are given;
his love endures for evermore:
give thanks to him, the God of heaven.

Metre: **88 88 (LM)**
O Righteous Lord; Gonfalon Royal

In a strange land

By foreign streams we sat and wept for Zion –
our tongues were stilled, our instruments unused;
how could we sing a holy song of worship
merely to keep our conquerors amused?

Lord, from the pain of homelessness and exile
we only ask for what is surely right:
remember those whose cruelty harmed our children,
and those who gladly ridiculed our plight.

How shall we sing the Lord's song in a strange land?
But if we will not praise, what are we worth?
In you we find our homeland and our hope, Lord;
you are our song, our greatest joy on earth.

Metre: **11 10 11 10**
Intercessor; Wyld (Betty Roe)

Unfailing purpose

What faithfulness, Lord, and what love you have
    shown!
My heart overflows as I bow at your throne;
no matter who hears me, nor what they believe,
I pour out my worship for you to receive.

Unparalleled honours belong to your name;
your word is exalted, unrivalled in fame:
that word was the message I needed to hear –
I prayed, and you helped me to conquer my fear.

Let all in authority listen to you
and lift up the offering of praise you are due:
for though you are far from those captive to pride,
you come to the lowly and walk by their side.

You hold me through trouble, secure in your hand:
my foes cannot rob me of what you have planned.
Lord, safe in your keeping, allow me to prove
your unfailing purpose, your unfailing love.

Metre: **11 11 11 11**
Datchet

Through and through

My Lord, you have examined me,
you know me through and through;
you see my deeds, perceive my thoughts,
my speech, my motives too.
You wrap me round on every side;
on me you place your hand:
such knowledge is too wonderful
for me to understand!

The presence of your Spirit will
be with me to the last;
wherever I decide to go
your love will hold me fast.
If I should try to run from you
I know without a doubt
no darkness could conceal my path –
your light would shine me out.

You made me in my mother's womb,
so intricate your ways,
and even then, before my birth,
you numbered all my days.
Before I sleep and as I wake
I know that you are there:
how could I ever sound the depths
of your unfailing care?

And yet I find my soul perturbed
by bitterness and grief,
for many choose to treat your word
with scornful unbelief –
so search me, Lord, and cleanse my heart
from all that you abhor,
then teach me how to walk with you
today and evermore.

Metre: **86 86 D (DCM)**
Kingsfold; Fordhouse (Michael Higgins)

Glad to honour you

Almighty Lord, your saints are glad
to honour you in songs of praise,
and eager to devote themselves
to walk with you throughout their days.

For when the needy are oppressed,
the poor and humble tossed aside,
you faithfully uphold the cause
of those who find their rights denied.

May wickedness succeed no more;
may slander reap its due reward;
may your protection be my shield –
you are my strength, all-powerful Lord.

From all who plan malicious snares,
whose bitter words engender strife,
from every heart intent on war,
I ask you to preserve my life.

With all your saints I, too, am glad
to honour you in songs of praise;
I eagerly renew my pledge
to walk with you throughout my days.

Metre: **88 88 (LM)**
Bow Brickhill; Gonfalon Royal

141　　Lord, make my prayer

Lord, make my prayer a sacrifice
like incense rising to your throne:
be mindful as I call for help;
be swift to make your answer known.

And make my prayer a hawk-eyed guard
who halts my lips from wicked speech;
who, when enticing evils lurk,
preserves my heart beyond their reach.

And make my prayer an open ear
to every kind rebuke you send:
Lord, never let me disregard
correction from a godly friend.

And make my prayer a force for change,
upholding right, opposing wrong,
till your word judges every thought
and your praise sounds from every tongue.

Lord, make my prayer a pledge of faith:
you see the trials along my way,
but all my hopes are set on you:
I trust myself to you today.

Metre: **88 88 (LM)**
Church Triumphant; Hereford

You know my way, the path I have to take;
you know each peril, every hidden snare;
you know the depths of loneliness I feel –
no one to walk with me, no one to care.

It is to you I come with my complaints,
to you I list my catalogue of woe:
Lord, with my spirit crushed and near despair,
I voice concerns that you already know.

Yet you are still my refuge, all I want,
my hope as long as I remain alive:
and now, pursued by strong and savage foes,
I need your help if I am to survive.

But when you break my soul's imprisonment
and I am found among the godly throng,
your kindness will inspire my gratitude,
and praise will be the essence of my song.

Metre: **10 10 10 10**
Go Forth (Michael Baughen)

Inclusive language variations
2.3 God, with my spirit crushed and near despair,

143   Always faithful

Holy God, I cry for mercy –
not that I deserve your care,
but, since you are always faithful,
hear my urgent prayer.

Once my heart was filled with wonder
at the marvels you had planned;
now my soul is thirsty for you
like a desert land.

An assailant now pursues me,
tries to snatch my hope away,
till my crushed and fainting spirit
trembles with dismay.

Do not turn your face against me:
life without your love is bleak.
Your deliverance, guidance, refuge –
these, my God, I seek.

By your love disarm my foes, Lord;
lead me through this time of strife;
gracious God, I am your servant,
now and all my life.

Metre: **87 85**
St Leonard's (Gould); Ingrave (Andrew Wright)

When battle clouds

When we face impending warfare
or when battle clouds the day,
you alone can give us wisdom
for the part we have to play;
when before the tide of history
mortal frailty stands revealed,
we depend on you to help us,
loving God, our Rock, our Shield.

Will you sit aloof and silent
while the nations rage and fight?
Will you tolerate injustice,
God whose ways are truth and light?
Will your mercy not deliver
those who turn to you in prayer?
Will there not be new songs written,
songs to thank you for your care?

When at last the conflict eases,
when these days of battle end,
may we share with all the nations
the abundant gifts you send;
then shall all our children flourish;
then our homes will be secured;
but our greatest joy and honour
will be knowing you, our Lord.

Metre: **87 87 D**
Bethany; Hyfrydol

Let us exalt

Let us exalt our King,
    offer our finest praise;
daily, and evermore,
    let us applaud his ways!
How right that he should be adored –
our great, unfathomable Lord.

Tell of his majesty,
    splendours of dazzling light;
speak of the awesome power
    shown in his acts of might!
As on these things we meditate,
how can we help but celebrate?

Under his gracious reign
    mercy will never fail;
anger is seldom found,
    kindness and love prevail:
his kingdom ever will endure,
a realm eternally secure.

Promises made – and kept;
    love which embraces all;
strength for the weary heart,
    courage for those who fall –
our God provides what each requires;
he loves to meet our hearts' desires.

Let us exalt our King,
    serve him in godly fear –
trusting his saving power,
    conscious that he is near.
How right it is to spread his fame!
Let every being praise his name!

Metre: **66 66 88**
Little Cornard; Sempringham (Elizabeth Hill)

With resounding alleluias,
all through life my soul shall raise
one unending song of worship,
one unceasing hymn of praise,
celebrating God Eternal,
Lord of everlasting days.

Even this world's noblest rulers –
rich or powerful, strong or brave –
will not give the help they promise
from the confines of the grave;
Jacob's God, our Hope, our Helper –
he alone is sure to save.

Praise the Lord, who formed the heavens,
shaped the land and filled the sea;
praise the Lord, whose heart for justice
treats the poor with equity;
praise the Lord for blind eyes opened,
praise for captive souls set free.

Sing to God, who thwarts the wicked,
gives the hungry food to share,
guards and guides the frightened stranger,
lifts the downcast from despair;
he upholds the weak and lonely –
praise him for such tender care!

With resounding alleluias,
all through life my soul shall raise
one unending song of worship,
one unceasing hymn of praise,
celebrating God Eternal,
Lord of everlasting days.

Metre: **87 87 87**
Rhuddlan

Inclusive language variations
2.6   is uniquely sure to save.
4.4-6   lifts the downcast from despair
        and upholds the weak and lonely –
        praise for such unrivalled care!

With hallelujahs honour God,
his wisdom and his might:
    you saints, extol the Righteous One
    who formed and named each star,
    who knows the pain of every wound,
    who heals the deepest scar,
who gathers exiles home again –
his praise is our delight.

Bring skilful tunes and thankful words:
for clouds that soar above,
    for food to nourish bird and beast,
    for every grassy hill;
    yet neither nature's finest joys
    nor human strength or skill
can bring the Lord such happiness
as hearts that trust his love.

He sends the snow – then at his word
the springtime is restored
    as icy blast and wintry chill
    succumb to warmth and life;
    but more than this, his word to us
    brings peace in place of strife;
you saints, let hallelujahs sound
in honour of the Lord.

Metre: **86 86 D (DCM)**
Kingsfold

Let all creation's wonders
    and countless angel hordes
unite in ceaseless worship
    to praise the Lord of lords:
he spoke, and formed the cosmos;
    he set the stars in place;
his voice defines the contours
    of interstellar space –
let sun and moon extol him
    and every planet sing;
across the constellations
    let alleluias ring.

From far beneath the oceans
    let joyful songs arise,
while hail and wind and lightning
    toss psalms across the skies.
You beasts of farm and jungle,
    let nature's hymn be heard;
tell out your maker's greatness,
    each insect, every bird;
you peoples and you rulers,
    acknowledge him as King –
from every generation
    let alleluias ring.

So let us lift our voices
    for all that we are worth
to God whose timeless splendour
    surpasses heaven and earth:
in love he chose and called us,
    a people of his own,
and gave to us a Saviour
    to make his mercy known.
His name alone we honour;
    our lifelong praise we bring;
from deep within our spirits
    let alleluias ring!

Metre: **76 76 Triple**
Thaxted; Zachary James (Norman Warren)

Let this honour

Sing of Yahweh's splendour! Gather to rejoice;
craft new songs of worship, people of God's choice;
praise the Lord your Maker, praise the Lord your
    King –
come with music, come with dancing, come to sing.
Those who humbly trust him, they are his delight:
let this honour be your joy both day and night.

Tell of Yahweh's splendour! Go to spread the word;
see that right around the globe the news is heard.
Warn of coming judgement; stress that grace is near;
challenge all the nations, bid their leaders hear.
God has made you heralds of salvation's way:
let this honour be your joy both night and day.

Metre: **11 11 11 11 11 11**
Armageddon; Rachie

See life as a psalm

Sing praise to the Lord, you people of grace;
fill heaven with the songs that sound from this place;
since you are God's servants and meet in his name,
his wonders declare and his glory proclaim.

His greatness exceeds what words can explain,
and his is the power no force can restrain;
with fanfares of horns and crescendos of strings
raise anthems to honour the King of all kings.

Where music is made, let rhythms abound:
let cymbals and drums add weight to the sound;
with dance that is graceful and words that are clear,
bring joy to the God you adore and revere.

Yield all that you are to worship the Lord –
see life as a psalm, each moment a chord;
let harmonies flourish and melodies soar –
let all that has breath praise the Lord evermore.

Metre: **10 10 11 11**
Laudate Dominum (Parry); Roseland (Simon Clark)

Notes

Psalm	Comment

Psalm   **Comment**

1   The first of the psalms focuses on a central tenet of Biblical discipleship: the need to meditate on, and be shaped by, God's word. Obedience is essentially seen in practice: a key word in this text is *signals*, in a line I owe to Fred Kaan.

2   In a multi-cultural, multi-faith society it is all too easy to think of Christianity as one more option in the selection of faiths. Psalm 2 puts a different perspective: our God is in control, and commands us to follow his way, revealed in Christ.

3   Many of the psalms were written not as theoretical praise songs but as reaffirmations of faith in the face of conflict. Sometimes our pressures are similar to those the psalmists faced, such as gossip, self-doubt, or family breakdown (see the psalm's title; hence stanza 1, lines 3-4).

4   The closing verse of Psalm 4 points to its potential for evening use; accordingly, here is a text also suitable for use in the evening, looking back over the day, resolving to let latent bitterness go, and refocusing on God before the night.

5   From an evening psalm to a morning one: and again, there are opportunities to search our own hearts. Verses 9-10 here lie behind stanza 3, to continue the train of thought from stanza 2 (verses 4-6); while verses 7-8 are the basis for stanza 4.

6   David's words in this psalm are a poignant reminder that not all our prayers are swiftly answered: *How long?* (verse 3). Yet still he trusts; and so can we, confident that our prayers are not ignored even if we do not yet know how God will respond. Hence the hope expressed in stanza 3.

7   Here is David probing honestly within his own soul: *if I have done this . . .* (verses 3-5; stanza 1, lines 4-8). So when he invokes his own integrity (verse 8) it is in that broader context (verse 9; stanza 2, lines 7-8); and his praise is offered to God because of God's own righteousness (verse 17; stanza 3, lines 7-8).

8   It is the thought of God's glory stamped throughout creation (verses 1, 9; cf Romans 1:20) which prompted the twin images of *a hallmark and a signature*. Stanza 2 is a response to the way young children, in particular, are enthusiastic for so many small things.

9   What does it mean to say that God is just? From Psalm 9, this text explores three important parts of the answer. It means that he stands with all who work for justice (eg verses 7-8); that he is a refuge for the downtrodden (verse 9); and that ultimately there is hope (verse 18).

10   The questions raised in the previous psalm are still evident; indeed, some traditions treat the two as one psalm. For this collection, however, they have given rise to two separate texts, both reaffirming trust in a good God.

11   As in many of the psalms, David's confidence here is grounded not in his own righteousness but in God, in whom he takes refuge. This is life lived with an awareness of God's constant, searching presence (verses 4-5) – hence the challenge of stanza 2.

12   Here is a cry which is so relevant for our society: the struggle of maintaining faith and integrity in a generation which devalues truth and even speech itself. This is a psalm for daily life!

13   The metre here is borrowed (with adaptation) from Fred Pratt Green's *Easter Day Carol*; the text begins from verse 2 of the psalm rather than verse 1, but thereafter follows the order of the biblical text.

14   Can a congregational hymn be written from a psalm which begins *The fool says in his heart, 'There is no God.'*? The book of Psalms gives two opportunities to address the question! This text aims to encourage some self-examination. See also Psalm 53.

Psalm	Comment
15	Psalm 15 remains highly challenging: the Lord looks for obedience from the heart, not ritual correctness. For verse 4, see stanza 3, lines 1-2. The final stanza echoes Matthew 7:24-27 – where the context is at least as challenging.
16	While this text does not follow the psalm as closely as some, I have tried to capture the main thrust: David's contentment in God, which is expressed now in delight in his people (v3) and for the future in hopes of a better eternity (verses 10-11; see Acts 2:27-28).
17	If this psalm looks like David indulging in self-righteous self-defence, perhaps we misunderstand him; perhaps the tone is more of self-examination to renew his assurance that the onslaught he faces is genuinely undeserved. Hence the general tenor of this text.
18	Psalm 18 is rich in vivid imagery and language, and I have tried to retain some of the colour of the original here. The shape of the text was inspired by Daniel Johnson's tune *Earth and All Stars*.
19	This psalm falls into three sections: God's glory revealed in creation, God's word, and a response of self-examination and commitment. This hymn text therefore has three verses.
20	Here the psalm is a blessing, pronounced over the hearer, whereas my text is a prayer for help. The four stanzas draw respectively on verses 1-3; verses 4-5 (with perhaps more than a glance towards the searching promise of Psalm 37:4); verses 6-7; and verses 6, 8 (with echoes of Matthew 6:19-21).
21	Derek Kidner (Tyndale OT Commentaries) says that this psalm could be 'a coronation ode . . . or for a royal anniversary' or celebrating a victory. This short text aims to draw on two of its underlying themes: God's generosity and his holy rule.
22	No Christian can approach Psalm 22 without being aware of Jesus on the cross. I hope this text can work at different levels: a meditation on the crucifixion, a personal plea for help, or a prayer for other believers in distress.
23	A particular problem in versifying the psalms comes from those which already have well-established hymn versions (23, 46, 72, 103, 104 . . .). This text is based on a modern Japanese version of Psalm 23 by Tokio Mogashio, which begins *The Lord is my pace-setter; I shall not rush*.
24	There is a slight re-ordering of the psalm in this text: the double assertion with which the psalm ends has provided the opening and closing stanzas, with both victory (verse 8) and glorious reign (verse 10) reflected in their respective final lines.
25	Although the underlying psalm here has an acrostic structure, I have simply followed the thread of thought through four stanzas. I know of no other text in this metre with the same rhyme scheme; which I find curious, since the rhyme pattern is not particularly unusual.
26	This psalm is not at all the same as the self-righteous Pharisee in Jesus' parable (Luke 18:9-14): the core of David's plea is trust (verse 2), delight in the Lord (verses 7-8) and a cry for mercy (verse 11). His obedience has become a gift of grace – hence the opening two lines of stanzas 1 and 5 here.
27	David's cry of commitment to God in the face of difficulty was no empty boast, and this psalm shows that he was aware of trouble from both enemies and family: yet still he would trust in God. In this text, each stanza sets the problems in the broader context of God's faithfulness and care.
28	The central portion of this psalm (verses 4-5) may look harsh and sub-Christian, yet the New Testament reinforces that there will be immeasurable loss for those whose hearts are closed to God. It is this thought which lies behind stanza 2 (especially lines 5-6) here.
29	When Michael Perry wrote *The God of heaven thunders* from Psalm 29, he emphasised the word *glory*. I found myself struck, by contrast, at how many times God's *voice* is mentioned, and it is that which shapes this text.

Psalm	Comment
30	Behind this psalm lies the kind of contentment of which Paul wrote (Philippians 4:11-13): the keynote is verses 6-7, which inspired stanza 3 of the text.
31	Here the first stanza of the text comes from verses 1-5; the second, more freely, from verses 6-8; the third, verses 9-13, again more freely; and the last two stanzas from verses 14-18 and verses 19-24 respectively, once again staying closer to the psalm.
32	Blessed is the person whose sin is forgiven, not the one who has achieved perfection (for who can?). This psalm is about the joy of repentance and forgiveness. Stanza 3, lines 1-4, put verse 6 in its broadest context.
33	This text follows the main thrust of the psalm, with the respective stanzas based on verses 1-3, 4-5, 6-9,10-11, 12-15, 16-19 and 20-22. The psalmist's breadth of vision is astonishing – so much is captured in so few lines!
34	David's exuberant acrostic psalm has yielded many riches, and my text cannot capture all of them. One of the best-known, from verse 8, seemed a fitting image to keep on one side and use for the climax of the text.
35	Here the underlying psalm is a plea from a persecuted believer for personal protection; the hymn text deliberately turns this around so that it becomes a prayer for the suffering church.
36	Psalm 36 has much in common with Proverbs; its challenges are whether we find ourselves listed among those whose faults it exposes and how we will respond. The key lines in this text are stanza 3, lines 5 and 6, which should always be our desire.
37	Like its predecessor, this psalm reflects much of the wisdom literature; here I have not retained the acrostic pattern of the psalm but have tried instead to draw out some of its main themes.
38	There are times when it feels as though we are utterly alone, with even God against us. Psalm 38 is a cry for such moments; this text aims to express something of the mixture of doubt, guilt and despair of which the Psalmist wrote.
39	Here is a psalm which begins with an outburst before moving into more measured reflection. For this text, however, I have taken stanza 1 from verses 4-6 and stanza 2 from verses 7-11, with verses 1-3 occurring only in stanza 3. The final stanza comes from verses 12-13.
40	There is more to this vibrant testimony than empty emotion: the writer recognises God's unique claims and the need for real obedience, not mere ritual; he also admits his continuing need for grace. I have tried to reflect all these thoughts in this text.
41	This is a fairly free rendition of Psalm 41, with the three stanzas broadly echoing verses 1-4, verses 5-9, verses 10-13. The key lines in these stanzas are, respectively, lines 5-6 (cf verse 3), lines 1-2 (cf verse 5), and lines 5-6 (from verses 11-12).
42, 43	This is the only hymn in this collection based on two psalms; but these two psalms certainly belong together! The text does not include the familiar imagery of the deer (Psalm 42:1) but does try to capture the mixture of joy and longing, sadness and hope.
44	Psalm 44 faces the difficult question of suffering: why is God not with us as he was with our ancestors, if we have not failed him? Verse 22 (cf Romans 8:36) opens a little insight into the wider plan of God; the end of my text tries to capture this.
45	This is a song for a royal wedding yet also a Messianic psalm, quoted in Hebrews 1. Put the two thoughts together, and the hope of the kingdom of God shines through. Stanza 4 (cf verses 10-15) therefore looks at the Church, Christ's bride.
46	The repeated assertion of God's presence (verses 7, 11) together with the reminder of who he is (verse 10), gave this text its shape. Although the psalm is solemn, it is also joyful; and perhaps the tune *Blessed Assurance* can reflect some of that joy.

Psalm	Comment
47	This is a psalm of exuberance, of awed worship and joyful song, of global vision and challenge to all the nations. Yet somehow the text was one which did not come at all easily, only reaching its finished state with considerable effort.
48	This psalm gives us a twofold picture of the presence of God, as shown in the holy city and in particular the temple. On the one hand, there is his awesome power (hence stanzas 1-2); on the other (stanzas 3-4), the beauty of his tender love.
49	The pithy wisdom of this psalm reaches a peak in verse 15, with its tantalising glimpse of hope beyond this life – however much or little the psalmist understood of it. Stanza 4 here picks up this thought in a free rendition loosely based on verses 12-15.
50	Stanza 1 here (from verses 1-6) sets the scene: God, the Holy One, pronounces judgement. He speaks of what he wants – not ritual, but obedience (verses 7-15; stanza 2) – and he challenges those who bring the former without the latter (verses 16-23; stanza 3).
51	While the title of this psalm dates it to one of David's darkest moments, its depth of penitence has far-reaching relevance. The bare simplicity of common metre seemed most fitting to such soul-searching.
52	On the surface, this psalm looks like no more than a vindictive outburst from a man who has been badly treated; but the climax of the psalm is a renewed trust in God's protection (verses 8-10) which yielded the opening stanza of this text as well as its ending.
53	From a psalm with a challenging opening come words which Paul quotes in Romans 3 as exemplifying human sinfulness. In this text, I have tried to acknowledge the temptation to 'practical atheism' – living without reference to God. See also Psalm 14.
54	Perhaps most of us never face literal threats to our lives in the same way that David did here, but there are Christians who do. A text like this may be one way to understand their struggles and hopes, and thus to pray for them more effectively.
55	Who could deny the contemporary relevance of a psalm which speaks of inner anguish, urban violence, alienation and the disintegration of friendship? In the midst of all this the Psalmist cries out to God in faith; this text tries to balance his pain and his hope.
56	Like several others in this collection, here is a text whose underlying structure comes from the psalm in question: the refrain in this text is found in verses 3-4 and again in verses 10-11. The text was written with the tune *Runciman* by Richard Runciman Terry in mind.
57	When surrounded by numerous foes (verse 4), David was confident that the Lord would be his defender, and therefore he expected to see his enemies routed (verse 6). Stanza 2 tries to reflect some of his confidence without trivialising or triumphalism.
58	Is this David the rebel castigating Saul's regime, or David the king chastising his own servants? Either way, the dangers of corrupt politics and the reality of accountability to God have a contemporary relevance. Here is a prayer for leaders – see 1 Timothy 2:1-2.
59	Here is a text which may only be of occasional use, perhaps to identify with persecuted Christians. The 'dogs' in the psalm did not prove as difficult to address as I feared, following some advice from Michael Forster.
60	Psalm 60 carries a sense of bewilderment and pain at turmoil which seems to be God's judgement, yet also the feeling that there is no real hope except in God. This text, though perhaps a freer rendition than some, tries to capture those thoughts.
61	This text was written in June 2001, and I am conscious that the image of a tower for a place of safety was greatly weakened only three months later. For the time being, though, I am reluctant to lose it completely.
62	Where do we turn when we are under attack? Rumour, gossip, and character assassination can be very real and potent difficulties. David's answer was to turn to God and seek his eternal perspective; hence this text.

Psalm	Comment

63   This is a psalm written in a desert by a man who knew the pain of an inward desert, yet who could still cry out with longing and hope to God. In stanza 3, I have taken verses 6-8 as indicative of David's low state of mind.

64   Once again the focus of this prayer is on speech, and the need for it to be godly and gracious. David's yearning (verses 7-8) is not mere party-politics ('God, be on my side') but a plea for justice; as I hope stanza 4 indicates.

65   In an age of mass-produced food, often grown overseas and transported great distances, it is easy to forget our reliance on God's provision. This psalm reminds us; this text might therefore be suitable for a harvest celebration.

66   Here are sufferings set in the context both of history (verses 5-6) and of God's dealings with us: in bringing us through the times of trial (verse 9) while also using them to refine us (verses 10-12). This text tries to follow the thread of the psalm.

67   This psalm captures so much of God's plan for the world: how his people should show his glory (verses 1-2) so clearly that all the earth would respond (verses 3-4) and learn to live in harmony with creation (verses 6-7). These three stanzas aim to express the yearning of the psalm.

68   My first text from this psalm was written in 1988; re-drafted 12 years later, it became this version. And though it begins with God's enemies being scattered (verses 1-2), by the end they are called to join the song of praise (verses 31ff).

69   This is one of those psalms containing some uncongenial elements, things which do not easily slot into contemporary Christian worship. I have tried to leave open the questions of whom we might count as enemies and what might become of them – see stanza 2. Even Christians can fall down here!

70   The tone of this particular text is set by verse 5a of the psalm, where David expresses his sense of weakness; hence stanza 1. Stanza 3 leans heavily on verses 4, 5b. The prayer for justice (verses 2-3) gives rise to stanza 2.

71   Some of the psalms provide their own clear structure: this is one example. The line used to close each stanza here is drawn from verses 8, 15 and 24 of the psalm; and the three stanzas are based on the sections delineated by those verses.

72   The Messianic nature of this psalm was clearly recognised by James Montgomery (1771-1854) in his hymn *Hail to the Lord's anointed*. I, too, have tried to reflect this same hope for the kingdom of Christ. This text can be sung to *Kelvingrove*.

73   Why do the righteous suffer while the wicked prosper? Many of us have struggled with that question. So did the Psalmist, who found some answers in God's presence in the temple. This text was drafted in mid-air, flying from Holland to the UK!

74   Like its predecessor, Psalm 74 bears witness to the struggle to understand suffering. A key word here is *remember* (verses 2, 18, 22); see stanzas 2 and 5. For some Christians, this kind of suffering is a daily reality; this, too, we should remember.

75   Psalm 75 celebrates the God who judges justly. A hymn should not be vindictive, so in this text I have tried to emphasise that God alone has the right to judge and chooses the time to do so; yet (stanza 4) we are still called to stand for righteousness.

76   I do not usually write hymn texts in one sitting; I have found that the result is often a poor final stanza in the rush to finish the writing. This text, however, was drafted in one sitting, while recuperating from minor surgery.

77   The fulcrum round which this psalm turns is verses 10-12, where the writer turns from his despair to look at God's acts in history. This is our heritage, too: here is a text which follows the same path to find hope.

Psalm	Comment
78	This is a long text – inevitably, perhaps, given the length of the psalm on which it is based, even though I have been brief in dealing with some sections. But as Paul wrote (1 Corinthians 10:6, 11) there are lessons for us here – hence stanza 1, lines 5-6.
79	Like some other texts in this volume, this is a prayer for those who face persecution for their faith in God. I have tried to capture something of the sense of desolation felt by those who originally used this psalm to cry out to God.
80	Although this psalm begins with the metaphor of a shepherd, it is the vine which is the central thought (verses 8-16). This lies behind stanza 3 of the hymn text. The refrain comes from verses 3, 7 and 19.
81	Psalm 81 is a celebration of God the deliverer, especially remembering the exodus, which ends with a call to holiness. My text looks at the deeper deliverance from sin (stanza 2) and the corresponding demands on our lives (stanza 3).
82	This is an enigmatic psalm, and Jesus' quotation of it (John 10:34) does not solve the enigma. For this text, I have taken the psalm as a courtroom scene where all of us find our values and behaviour challenged by the demands of holiness.
83	The thesis of Psalm 83 is: Lord, you have delivered in times past; do so again now. For many believers, this need for help is a daily reality. Stanza 3 interprets verses 9-12 in the light of Ephesians 6:12.
84	In stanza 1 here (based on verses 1-4) I have inadvertently used a rhyme which David Preston also employed in his setting of this psalm. Stanza 3 builds on verses 10-12 but rearranges the order a little.
85	Like Psalm 83, this is a song for heart-searching: why do we no longer enjoy God's blessings as once we did? There are times when we, too, need to renew our resolve to follow the Lord; this psalm and this text are for such times.
86	This is another psalm with a broad scope and vision: from real personal troubles (verses 1-7, 14) to a global vision of God's glory (verses 8-10, 15) and a renewed determination to serve and praise the Lord (verses 11-13, 16-17). The hymn text tries to mirror this – though necessarily omitting some of the detail.
87	Zion (verses 2, 5, 6): originally the name of the hill, then another name for Jerusalem, and a metaphor for God's people. Now the term has political overtones and must be used carefully. This text does not include it; but the image of the city of God remains powerful, and occurs in the New Testament as well.
88	While this psalm is not immediately obvious as congregational material – not least because it expresses the very personal anguish of isolation – there must be a space for such feelings in corporate worship. For how many in the average congregation are fully immune to such turmoil?
89	This long psalm recounts some of Israel's history and draws painful and pertinent lessons from it. Inevitably, four stanzas of eight lines each cannot contain all that is in the psalm; I hope there is enough to capture a little of the original feeling.
90	Two key themes of Psalm 90 are *refuge* and *hope*, and I have used both in this text, originally drafted from the Jerusalem Bible. Stanza 1 comes from verses 1-2 and stanza 4 from verses 14-17; stanzas 2 and 3 are derived more freely from verses 3-13.
91	Psalm 91, quoted out of context by Satan to Jesus in the wilderness temptations, does not justify a glib approach to suffering. I hope this text is true to the fuller biblical perspective: help through troubled times, and ultimate, eternal security.
92	This text is built on five phrases: *how good* (stanza 1, from verses 1-3 of the psalm); *how glad* (stanza 2, from verses 4-5); *how many* (stanza 3, echoing verses 6-9, 11); *how gracious* (stanza 4, drawing on verses 10, 12-15); and, as verse 15 is echoed in the final line of the text, *how right*.

Psalm	Comment
93	Psalm 93 proved surprisingly resistant to versification. Eventually I settled on the pattern of echoing (not directly repeating) the first line of each stanza in the corresponding last line; a little like the structure of the psalm itself.
94	This text is based on Psalm 94, as expounded by Tom Wright in *Small faith, great God*. Seeing God's discipline in hardship is a valuable lesson to learn (Hebrews 12:7); the key lines in this text are the final couplet of stanza 2.
95	The invitation to *come* in verses 1 and 6 of this psalm gave this text a fairly obvious structure; it seems to me that the same invitation is implied in verses 7-8, where we are called to still our hearts before God's solemn word.
96	Here is praise which is in no way hollow or flippant in a psalm which mingles joy and reverence, recognising and responding to the holy God. Stanza 4, lines 1-2, are from verse 13; the remainder of that stanza, verses 11-12.
97	Two key thoughts here are very relevant for today: the challenge of other religions (verse 7, cf stanza 3, lines 1-2); and the call to holy living (verse 10, cf stanza 4, lines 1-2). Both challenges are a response to the greatness and holiness of God.
98	Do we need new hymns and songs? The opening line of this psalm still encourages us to craft them; and the task of shaping praise for a new generation, expressing unchanging truth in fresh ways, is as exhilirating and demanding as ever.
99	Here is a straightforward treatment of Psalm 99: the repeated last line comes from verses 3, 5 and 9, the respective stanzas follow verses 1-3, verses 4-5, verses 6-7 and verses 8-9 fairly closely.
100	In this text the key is found in the fifth lines, where the first stanza echoes verse 3 and the second stanza, verse 5. These are fundamentally two of the great reasons to praise God: the response should include both joy and reverence.
101	Do we have David's rigorous determination to live by God's holiness every day? He was determined not to indulge in evil, not to listen to slander, and not to tolerate deceit; we could do worse than this! Here is a text to reflect his longing.
102	This is a lament, a cry of pain. Stanza 1 builds from verses 1-11, trying to capture the sense of desolation felt by the psalmist; stanza 2 (verses 12-18) refocuses on God; stanza 3 (verses 19-28) tries to resolve the two thoughts in the context of eternity.
103	I have no wish to usurp the honoured place in hymnody held by Henry Francis Lyte's text from Psalm 103. However, these stanzas offer an alternative view of a much-loved psalm; if the metre looks unfamiliar, try humming *Greensleeves* …
104	One question which arose when drafting this text was how to deal with the cosmology in verse 5: the Psalmist could see less of the earth's place in the galaxy than we can; a contemporary understanding is reflected in line 1 of stanza 2.
105	Our heritage includes the patriarchs, the exodus and the wilderness wanderings: here are a psalm and a hymn text which reflect that fact. I have not tried to list seven of the plagues (as the psalm does, verses 28-36) but have summarised these verses in stanza 3, lines 5-8.
106	Before and after this psalm we have celebrations of God's goodness through history; this is the darker side, the disobedience of his people. This, too, is our history – hence stanzas 2, 3 and 7.
107	For this more song-like text I have followed the broad sweep of the psalm in reflecting God's deliverance seen in a variety of situations – we may all be able to identify with some of them. Verses 33-38 are alluded to in stanzas 2 and 5.
108	It is always good to be reminded that *all* the nations of the world are in God's hands; and while we may not have the same territorial agendas as our Old Testament forebears, we still have a task (stanza 4, lines 1-2) for which we need God's help.

Psalm	Comment
109	This is a 'difficult' psalm; Peter even applies its curses to Judas Iscariot (Acts 1:20). Taking the NIV footnote reading (that verses 6-19 are quoting the venom which David faced), stanzas 2 and 3 are here cast as false charges; and Christians can face such tests of faith.
110	I did not try to include Melchizedek in this text (though other writers, such as Emma Turl, have managed it). I have also drawn on Hebrews 7:1, 3 to illuminate the less obvious aspects of this Messianic psalm.
111	For this exuberant psalm I have revisited a metre and a tune I had not used for some time: *Stowey*. Verse 7 looks back to the exodus; in my text, the parallel is stanza 2, line 2, with a reminder that God is still sovereign over all the nations.
112	This is another psalm which covers a vast range of thought and echoes the style of Proverbs. For this text the opening word was difficult: *blessed* seems too 'religious', and *happy* too ambiguous. No ambiguity over the tune I had in mind: *Lobe Den Herren*.
113	It is good to know that the Lord who reigns over all the earth and controls all the nations is intimately interested in the details of our lives. This text is a straightforward setting of the psalm.
114	Line 2 of the first stanza of this text contains a phrase which is not found in Psalm 114 at all; however, Israel's experiences of Egypt contained enough oppression to make the image pertinent. The remainder of the text is closer to the psalm.
115	What a contrast there is in this psalm between the living God and the hollow claims of the idols! What are the idols of our generation? The living God still calls people to follow and to serve him; see stanza 3, based loosely on verses 9-13.
116	Here is the psalmist rejoicing in life, and in having been delivered from death by God's mercy; yet having learned, too, that God cares about what happens to his people – see verse 15, echoed in the penultimate line of the text.
117	From the shortest of the psalms, a song text rather than a hymn. Even in these two short verses the psalmist gives us both good reason and great encouragement to praise the Lord.
118	It was intriguing to study Psalm 118 with a view to writing a text, and to see how themes emerge and develop through the psalm. The text, when it finally came together, followed the main thread of the psalm.
119a	Rather than try to versify the whole of Psalm 119, I attempted to find some recurring themes, and it is these which lie behind the three stanzas of this text . . .
119b	. . . but having written one text on Psalms 42 and 43, I recognised that I would have 149 texts on 150 psalms, which would irritate me! To resolve the problem I revisited Psalm 119, selected three stanzas of the psalm, and wrote this text from those verses.
120	Words are powerful; and in an age of spin, half-truth, advertising excesses and broken promises, integrity in speech is a real issue of discipleship for many Christians. I hope this text captures something of the Psalmist's struggles in this area.
121	Two comments are needed here. Stanza 1 reflects Michael Saward's comment that the psalm begins by asserting that whatever is offered by the hills (or the idols worshipped there), it is not here but to God that we turn for help. And verses 7-8 are interpreted in the broader context; see Romans 8:28.
122	For the Psalmist, Jerusalem was a physical destination, ideally three times a year. We may think instead of a spiritual Jerusalem (see Hebrews 12:22), but the same emphasis on building community still holds good for the Church.
123	There is an interesting insight here on the biblical relationship of master and servant: the servant looks to the master not only for instruction but also for protection. This text contains both aspects, in stanzas 2 and 3 respectively.

Psalm	Comment

Psalm *Comment*

124   I have tried in this text to reflect something of the mood of the psalm, as well as its vivid imagery. That mood seems simply to be one of grateful relief at being rescued from a perilous situation. It is a sentiment many of us can echo!

125   Here verse 3 reminds us that God is active within history, an insight confirmed in the New Testament (eg Matthew 24:22): who knows what unseen protection we enjoy, from both evil forces and temptations?

126   Memory can be an interesting thing: in this psalm we have both a reliving of past joys and a wistful yearning to feel those same joys again. The tune *Royal Oak*, with its balance of exuberance and reflection, seems appropriate for such a text.

127   Psalm 132 builds on two meanings of the word *house*; it seems to me that the same idea illuminates Psalm 127. Here, therefore, is a text which talks of houses as both buildings (stanza 1) and families (stanza 2).

128   This is a simple psalm, looking at what it means to walk in God's ways (verse 1). I have tried to pick up many of the threads here: the real value of work and health (verse 2), home and family (verse 3), peace at every level (verses 5-6) and a full life (verse 6).

129   I remember this being a difficult text to write: not only is the imagery of the psalm less than crystal-clear; its sentiments do not easily lend themselves to congregational song. Nevertheless, the psalmist has a strong testimony about God's faithfulness and justice in his dealings with his people, and the text draws on this.

130   The psalmist moves from near-despair (verses 1-2, stanza 1) through an awareness of God's mercy (verses 3-4, stanza 2) to a climax of hope with growing confidence. This text was one of the earliest I wrote, though it was revised later.

131   The challenge of Psalm 131 is the call to find contentment in God and in small things: and if David, with all the burdens of royal responsibility, could feel such peace, who are we to ask for more? This text was drafted fairly quickly.

132   As noted above (see Psalm 127) this psalm is built on a pun. The use of a long tune such as *Thaxted* enabled me to shape the text in two stanzas to reflect this structure; but also to draw out some of the Messianic implications of verses 17-18.

133   I have long been wary of the word 'blessing', fearing that it has become a piece of religious jargon which we use without really thinking about its meaning; hence the freer rendition in the final two lines of this short text.

134   This short text from a short psalm was the last to be drafted for this collection. The words pick up Erik Routley's phrase 'duty and delight'; the music which I had in mind as I wrote was Caryl Micklem's delightful tune *Gatescarth*.

135   Modern ears and minds are uncomfortable about verses 8-12, but the Psalmist saw God's hand at work releasing slaves, judging wickedness and giving his people a long-promised home. Stanza 3 tries to capture this.

136   The shape of this text is heavily influenced by the recurrent refrain of the psalm: the never-ending, never-failing love of God, creator, deliverer, provider. Successive stanzas address those different pictures; but all include that refrain.

137   Here I have taken the verses of the psalm in a different order for the hymn text, with stanza 2 using verses 7-10 and stanza 3, verses 4-6. In the former case, the vindictiveness of the original becomes a cry for justice from the context of pain.

138   David had a great vision of God as King of all the earth, one which made him eager to see the Lord praised in every land and instead of all other gods. This vision remains vital and challenging in our multi-faith world – hence stanza 1, lines 3-4.

139   This text, originally drafted in August 1987, was my first hymn-text. It was subsequently revised but retains much of its original character. For more details, see the Introduction.

Psalm	Comment
140	However uncomfortable we feel with forthright denunciations like those in verses 8-11 of this psalm, they serve as a reminder that justice is part of God's purpose for the world. Stanza 2 of this text reiterates that; and stanza 3 prays for its fulfilment.
141	David specifically likens his prayer to incense in verse 1, and speaks of its power for opposing sin in verse 5; it struck me that several other aspects of prayer were at least implied in the sentiments of the other verses of the psalm. Hence this text.
142	Here is another cry from a low point; there is a contrast with Psalm 57, a more buoyant psalm from the same circumstances. Yet David remained wise enough to cry to God rather than wallowing in despair. This text tries to capture both his complaint and his faith.
143	Although the Psalmist does not say it in so many words, the central conviction of this prayer is that life without God's love is bleak (stanza 4, line 2); nothing else can restore and reinvigorate the thirsty heart, whether the immediate woe is internal (verses 4-6) or outward (verses 3,12).
144	At the time I drafted this text in January 2003, widespread heartsearching over looming war in Iraq gave these words a context and a relevance I had not envisaged. Sadly, there will doubtless be many more situations when it might prove appropriate.
145	This was one of my earliest hymn texts, written with *Little Cornard* in mind, and subsequently revised. I have been challenged over stanza 3, line 3, but maintain that this is a fair inference from verse 8 of the psalm.
146	Having drafted this text, I was intrigued to find that, by joining the opening and closing thoughts of the psalm in a repeated first/last stanza, I had done the same as Isaac Watts (*I'll praise my Maker while I've breath*).
147	This is another psalm which ranges widely in looking to God as creator, redeemer, and provider: the infinite God, the intimate God. The text follows the psalm, but with a slightly unusual rhyme scheme.
148	Written with Gustav Holst's tune *Thaxted* in mind, and based on the lavish and exuberant praises of Psalm 148, this text remains one of my own favourites from the whole collection.
149	This psalm falls into two parts which balance each other: the call to come and praise (verses 1-5) and the call to go in God's service (verses 6-9). In the light of the New Testament, the latter is the call to mission – which includes declaring the truth and warning of judgement.
150	So ends the Psalter, with another outburst of triumphant praise; in a free paraphrase of verse 6 here, I have tried to encourage the idea that the whole of life should be an offering of praise. Hence the final stanza of this final psalm text.

Thematic Index by Psalm Number

Theme	Psalm	Theme	Psalm	Theme	Psalm
Aaron	77, 99	Companionship	23	Discipleship	1, 15, 16, 26,
Abraham	105	Compassion	41, 82, 147		36, 37, 40, 41,
Abundance	67, 72	Complaints	142		42/43, 53, 61,
Accountability	10	Compromise	120		79, 84, 97, 101,
Accusation	71, 109	Condemnation	41, 109		105, 115, 118,
Adoration	95, 96, 134,	Confession	32, 38, 51, 80		119a, 128, 140,
	148, 150	Confidence	27, 70, 71, 86		141
Agony	6	Conflict	7, 10, 41,	Discipline	39, 89, 94, 102
Agreement	133		42/43, 56, 58,	Disgrace	44, 69
Allegiance	81, 123		59, 69, 70, 71,	Dismay	143
Ambition	20, 115, 131		83, 86, 91, 120,	Disobedience	78
Angels	34, 35, 99		128, 129, 143,	Distress	38
Anger	89		144	Diversity	122
Anguish	6, 38, 42/43,	Conqueror	24	Doubt	13, 22, 74, 77
	77, 86, 102	Conscience	7, 53	Dreams	115
Animals	8, 104, 148	Conspiracy	64	Dryness	42/43, 63
Anxiety	13, 55, 63, 88,	Constellation	148	Duty	134
	143	Contempt	131		
Arrogance	10, 12, 36, 101,	Contentment	131	Earth	104
	120, 123	Contrition	51	Egypt	103, 105, 114,
Assistance	124, 143	Conviction	15, 38		135
Atheism	10, 14, 53	Correction	94, 141		
Attitude	15	Cosmos	148	Emptiness	63
Authorities	47	Courage	31	Enemies	7, 17, 54, 56,
Awe	39	Covenant	23, 44, 46, 74,		57, 62, 86
			103, 105, 116,	Environment	104
Barrenness	63		132, 145, 149	Eternity	21, 49, 62, 73,
Battle	144	Creation	8, 19, 33, 65,		90, 93, 102,
Believers	35		67, 95, 96, 97,		116
Belonging	87, 107, 149		98, 104, 114,	Ethics	53
Betrayal	3, 55, 70		135, 139, 146,	Evangelism	107
Bible	1, 19, 119a,		147, 148	Evening	4
	119b, 138	Creator	33, 65, 67, 74	Evil	7, 58, 83, 94,
Birth	39	Crisis	53, 59, 60		129
Blame	41	Cynicism	12	Exile	78, 137
Blasphemy	74			Exodus	66, 105, 114,
Bleakness	88	Dance	149, 150		135, 136
Boasting	12, 64	Danger	3, 54, 56, 91,	Exploitation	10
Body	139		121, 142, 143	Faith	9, 11, 15, 22,
Body of Christ	35, 122	Darkness	88		25, 42/43, 55,
Bride of Christ	45	David	78, 89, 132		56, 59, 63, 74,
Bridegroom	45	Day	104		87, 112, 118,
Brutality	74, 124	Day of Judgement	110		123, 141
Busyness	23	Death	39, 86, 116	Faithfulness	44, 46, 57, 63,
		Deceit	12, 26, 36		66, 73, 86, 100,
Calamity	60	Decision	23, 25, 53		103, 105, 111,
Calmness	23	Defence	109, 124		117, 130, 138,
Canaan	106	Deliverance	18, 28, 34, 40,		143, 145
Captivity	126		54, 56, 64, 66,	Falsehood	9, 12, 120
Care	68, 69, 91, 94,		70, 71, 86, 91,	Fame	49, 75
	100, 113, 121		126, 135, 136,	Family	27, 112, 113,
Celebration	81, 95, 98, 117		143		115, 127, 128,
Children	8, 112, 127,	Dependence	44		133
	128	Depression	13, 30, 88	Fear	13, 27, 30, 60,
Children of God	87	Desert	78		88, 91, 102,
Choice	11, 23, 25	Desolation	88		115
Christ's sufferings	22	Despair	4, 9, 22, 28, 30,	Fellowship	122, 133
Church	45, 87		55, 77, 88, 116,	Flattery	12
City	55, 127		142, 146	Foes	62
Climate	135, 147	Desperation	60	Forgiveness	19, 25, 32, 51,
Comfort	6, 41, 86, 90,	Destiny	37, 49		65, 103, 130
	123, 137	Destitute	146	Fraud	7
Commandments	119b	Destruction	74	Freedom	68, 81, 107,
Commitment	16, 26, 37, 40,	Devotion	140		126, 136
	61, 97, 101,	Difficulty	20, 74	Friends	122
	108, 116, 118,	Dignity	3	Fruitfulness	23, 41, 92
	140, 141	Discernment	119a	Future	27, 31, 108

Theme	Psalm	Theme	Psalm	Theme	Psalm
Generosity	103, 112	Idolatry	106		93, 96, 97, 108,
Gifts	21, 65	Idols	97, 115, 135		111, 145
Gladness	100	Illness	41	Marginalised	82
Glory	8, 18, 24, 57,	Influence	127	Martyrdom	79
	97, 113, 148,	Injustice	9, 10, 72, 79,	Meditation	1
	150		94, 109, 137,	Meekness	75
Goals	20		140	Melchizedek	110
Gold	49	Innocent	10	Melody	150
Goodness	129	Instruments	150	Memory	42/43, 63, 77
Gospel	149	Insults	69	Mercy	26, 30, 38, 51,
Government	58, 125	Integrity	17, 27, 41, 101		52, 80, 85, 106,
Grace	5, 32, 47, 80,	Isaac	105		130
	84, 85, 108,	Isolation	38, 102	Messiah	2, 45, 72, 132
	130, 134, 149	Israel	77, 78, 105,	Mission	107
Gratitude	65, 66, 92, 96,		106, 135, 136	Money	121
	116, 118, 136,			Mortality	39, 49, 53, 73,
	142	Jacob	75, 77		146
Grave	33	Jerusalem	122, 125	Moses	77, 99, 105,
Greatness	93	Jordan	114		106
Greed	10	Joseph (Genesis)	77, 105	Motives	109
Guidance	16, 31, 32, 53,	Joy	14, 16, 22, 39,	Music	98, 149, 150
	119a, 143		81, 92, 100,	Nations	2, 46, 47, 58,
Guilt	25, 32, 38, 51,		114, 115, 134		60, 67, 76, 111,
	85	Judgement	2, 5, 7, 9, 11,		117, 144
			21, 32, 34, 36,		
Habit	81		50, 73, 75, 76,	Nature	65, 147, 148
Harassment	35		80, 82, 92, 94,	Night	4, 104
Hardship	70, 74, 79, 129,		96, 98, 106,		
	137, 142		110, 120, 129,	Obedience	15, 40, 50, 81,
Harmony	133, 150		141, 149		86, 95, 111,
Harvest	65	Judgements	119b		112, 119b
Haven	57	Justice	7, 9, 10, 11, 14,	Offering	50
Health	128		33, 34, 36, 45,	Omniscience	139
Heart	4, 14, 26, 33		55, 56, 58, 67,	Opposition	35, 59, 69, 79,
Heartache	6		69, 72, 73, 76,		109, 124, 129
Heaven	16, 69, 81, 87,		79, 82, 94, 97,	Oppression	76
	115		99, 109, 112,	Outcast	69
Help	18, 20, 22, 28,		122, 125, 137,	Outsider	146
	64, 70, 124,		140, 144, 146		
	141, 143, 144			Pain	22, 39, 42/43
Heritage	37, 61, 105	Kindness	111	Panic	53, 56
Hiding-place	2	Kingdom	2, 45, 46, 72,	Pardon	32, 107
History	9, 77, 78, 106,		89, 93, 96, 117,	Parenthood	127
	136, 144		132, 145	Passion	22
Holiness	5, 14, 15, 21,	Kingship	24, 72	Past	25
	24, 26, 33, 50,	Knowledge	119a, 139	Patience	123
	80, 81, 82, 83,			Patriarchs	105
	93, 99, 112,	Labour	127	Peace	17, 21, 29, 30,
	125, 135, 141	Law	2, 19, 93, 99,		32, 37, 46, 69,
Holy Spirit	32		119a, 119b		76, 116, 122,
Homage	47, 50, 76	Leaders	58, 146		125, 127, 128,
Home	113, 126, 128,	Learning	49, 49		131, 133, 144,
	137	Lies	12, 101, 120		147
Homelessness	137	Life	16, 39, 103	Peacemaking	120
Honesty	17, 36	Lifespan	62, 90	Penitence	51, 80, 85
Honour	18	Lifestyle	15, 26, 34, 40,	People of God	87
Hope	6, 9, 17, 20, 22,		41, 52, 61, 101,	Peoples	67, 117
	27, 31, 39, 60,		128	Peril	121, 142
	69, 73, 89, 90,	Light	119a	Persecution	35, 69, 74, 79,
	102, 103, 116,	Listening	95		137
	119b, 123, 129,	Loneliness	88, 102, 113,	Perseverance	84, 129
	142		142	Perspective	73
Hostility	59	Longing	42/43, 63	Pilgrimage	84, 122
Humanity	8, 110, 139	Love	33, 36, 40, 48,	Poor	10, 82, 94, 113,
Humiliation	44		52, 89, 100,		140, 146
Humility	75, 85, 131,		101, 103, 118,	Poverty	82
	138		133, 136, 138,	Power	111
Hunger	63		143	Praise	18, 33, 45, 47,
Hymns	98				52, 68, 86, 96,
Hypocrisy	26	Majesty	8, 50, 76, 89,		98, 100, 103,

Theme	Psalm	Theme	Psalm	Theme	Psalm
	108, 111, 113, 117, 137, 145, 146, 148, 149, 150	Riches	16, 21, 49, 52, 62, 75, 121	Spite	4
		Right and wrong	11, 53	Splendour	8, 50, 84, 93, 97, 148
Prayer	5, 6, 9, 13, 18, 20, 21, 28, 30, 35, 53, 66, 79, 112, 141	Righteousness	7, 14, 28, 33, 36, 37, 45, 50, 67, 85, 97, 99, 111	Steadfastness	112
				Stewardship	8, 67
		Rights	140	Stranger	146
Presence of God	5, 27, 28, 46, 48, 52, 53, 65, 79, 84, 87, 91, 114, 134, 135, 139	Ritual	50	Strength	3, 18, 23, 28, 84, 86, 128
		Rivers	104		
		Rock	95	Stress	4, 38
		Rulers	47, 58, 82, 125, 146	Strife	55, 140
Pressure	3, 41, 112, 120			Success	20
Pride	75, 76, 101, 131, 138	Safety	3, 11, 17, 35, 48, 56, 61, 62, 66, 91, 118, 121, 124, 125, 131	Suffering	22, 44, 73, 79, 102, 129, 137
Priesthood	110, 135			Superpowers	108
Problems	4, 70, 71			Survival	142
Proclamation	149	Saints	35		
Promise	81, 89, 91, 105, 119a, 119b, 132	Salvation	18, 31, 49, 54, 67, 68, 71, 81, 90, 112, 126, 149	Teaching	19
				Temple	48, 132
Promised Land	106, 114	Samuel	99	Temptation	83, 141
Prophecy	132	Sanctuary	28, 78	Tenderness	103
Prosperity	72	Satisfaction	1	Terror	55
Protection	11, 16, 25, 28, 31, 34, 35, 37, 48, 52, 53, 54, 56, 57, 59, 61, 62, 64, 71, 84, 91, 118, 124, 125, 136, 143	Savagery	74	Testimony	34, 40, 107, 108
		Saviour	95		
		Scorn	44, 123	Thankfulness	92, 136
		Scripture	1, 19, 119a, 119b, 138	Thanksgiving	30, 34, 65, 92, 100, 116, 118, 126
		Sea	104		
		Seasons	104, 135, 147	Thirst	42/43
Provision	65, 67, 68, 104, 144, 145	Second Coming	110	Thoughts	4, 13, 51
		Secrets	33	Threats	35, 54, 64
Psalms	150	Security	3, 4, 17, 21, 27, 30, 31, 37, 46, 56, 57, 61, 62, 71, 89, 91, 108, 121, 124, 125, 127, 131, 137, 138, 139, 144	Throne	24, 48
Punishment	95			Time	90, 102
Purpose	138			Toil	128
				Tongue	5
Questioning	74			Tragedy	66
				Trauma	57
Reassurance	77			Treachery	125
Red Sea	114			Treasure	16
Refreshment	23, 119a			Trials	44, 70
Refuge	2, 7, 9, 11, 16, 28, 39, 46, 57, 59, 60, 61, 62, 71, 90, 91, 142, 143	Seeking God	5	Triumph	2, 6, 24, 44, 48, 60, 63, 68, 89, 110, 129
		Service	115		
		Shalom	133		
		Shelter	91	Troubles	3, 20, 31, 70, 71
		Shepherd	95		
Refugees	147	Sin	14, 15, 19, 21, 32, 38, 50, 51, 52, 73, 75, 82, 85, 106, 130	Trust	1, 4, 11, 13, 17, 20, 22, 25, 27, 31, 33, 37, 42/43, 54, 55, 56, 57, 59, 62, 63, 71, 118, 123, 143, 145
Reign	2, 24, 145				
Rejection	74				
Rejoicing	92, 100, 117				
Reliance	20	Singing	150	Truth	12, 29, 36, 40, 45, 96, 101, 119a, 119b, 120
Relief	6	Skills	20		
Renewal	14, 126	Slander	15, 41, 64, 101, 109, 140		
Repentance	7, 15, 51, 80, 85	Sleep	3, 4	Turmoil	59, 77
		Social justice	82	Tyranny	125
Rescue	18, 34, 40, 64, 66, 107, 124	Society	58, 127	Tyrant	72, 125
		Sorrow	6, 13, 42/43		
Resources	20	Sovereignty	2, 21, 33, 47, 53, 58, 60, 66, 93, 99, 102, 108, 111, 113, 115, 121, 125, 135, 138	Unbelief	78
Responsibility	8			Uncertainty	30
Rest	95			Understanding	25, 147
Restoration	80			Ungodliness	52
Restraint	120			Unity	122, 133
Resurrection	17			Universe	8
Revelation	83				
Reverence	29, 66, 97, 98, 100, 114	Space	104, 148	Vanity	39
		Speech	12, 120	Victims	9, 10, 72
Revival	14, 126	Spirit of God	32	Victory	24, 44, 68, 89, 110
Rhythm	150	Spiritual warfare	83, 141		

Theme	Psalm	Theme	Psalm	Theme	Psalm
Vindication	11, 17, 35, 54, 57, 109	Wilderness	78, 106	Work	127, 128
		Wildlife	104	Worship	33, 47, 66, 76,
Vine	80	Will of God	5, 115		98, 132, 134,
Violence	55, 58	Wisdom	16, 18, 19, 36,		138, 148, 149
Voice of God	29, 83		49, 53, 78, 104,		
Vow	61		111, 119b	Worthlessness	3
		Witness	19, 40, 51, 107,		
Warfare	76, 120, 140,		108, 145	Wounds	147
	144	Word (Bible)	1, 19, 29, 68,	Wrath	80, 88
Wealth	21, 26, 49, 52,		83, 119a, 138,		
	62, 75, 121,		147		
	127	Words	12, 64	Zion	48, 132

Metrical Index by Psalm Number

Meter	Psalm	Meter	Psalm	Meter	Psalm
4 10 6 6 6 6 4 10	21	77 77 77	55	88 88 (LM)	49
66 6 D	101	77 77 77	88	88 88 (LM)	63
66 66	128	77 77 77 refrain 77	80	88 88 (LM)	74
66 66	133	77 77 D	36	88 88 (LM)	122
66 66 44 8	2	84 84 88 84	70	88 88 (LM)	136
66 66 88	28	85 85 87	119b	88 88 (LM)	140
66 66 88	68	86 86 (CM)	14	88 88 (LM)	141
66 66 88	78	86 86 (CM)	20	88 88 87 87	22
66 66 88	145	86 86 (CM)	27	88 88 88	39
66 84	5	86 86 (CM)	51	88 88 88	60
66 84 D	29	86 86 (CM)	75	88 88 88	85
66 84 D	113	86 86 (CM)	83	88 88 88	92
66 84 D	115	86 86 (CM)	106	88 88 88	125
66 86 (SM)	4	86 86 (CM)	120	8 8 8 10	13
66 86 (SM)	61	86 86 (CM)	124	8 11 9 33 7	117
66 86 (SM)	82	86 86 86	23	97 99 7	116
66 86 (SM)	123	86 86 D (DCM)	57	98 98 D	7
66 86 (SM)	131	86 86 D (DCM)	90	98 98 D	40
66 86 D (DSM)	79	86 86 D (DCM)	139	98 98 D	69
66 86 D (DSM)	100	86 86 D (DCM)	147	99 99 refrain 99 99	46
67 67 66 66	110	86 86 88	52	99 99 99	107
74 74 D	96	86 86 88 86	44	9 10 9 10 8 9	18
76 76	126	86 88 6	134	10 4 10 4	66
76 76 76	48	8 77 D refrain 8 77	73	10 8 10 8	121
76 76 D	1	87 85	143	10 10 10 4	99
76 76 D	9	87 87 Iambic	86	10 10 10 10	12
76 76 D	19	87 87 447	16	10 10 10 10	87
76 76 D	32	87 87 44 77	58	10 10 10 10	97
76 76 D	35	87 87 67	3	10 10 10 10	114
76 76 D	59	87 87 77	38	10 10 10 10	118
76 76 D	65	87 87 87	77	10 10 10 10	142
76 76 D	95	87 87 87	146	10 10 10 10 10 10	94
76 76 Triple	42	87 87 D	34	10 10 10 10 10 10	102
76 76 Triple	43	87 87 D	71	10 10 11 11	11
76 76 Triple	132	87 87 D	81	10 10 11 11	150
76 76 Triple	148	87 87 D	84	11 10 11 10	53
76 76 77 76	72	87 87 D	89	11 10 11 10	67
76 76 77 76	127	87 87 D	98	11 10 11 10	76
76 77	54	87 87 D	109	11 10 11 10	104
76 77	130	87 87 D	129	11 10 11 10	137
76 86 D	41	87 87 D	144	11 10 11 10 11 10	50
77 76	45	87 87 D refrain 87 87	56	11 10 11 10 11 10	119a
77 77	6	88 86	26	11 10 11 10 11 10 11 12	105
77 77	30	88 86 7 10 77	103	11 11	33
77 77	62	88 88 D (DLM)	37	11 11 11 11	31
77 77	64	88 88 D (DLM)	91	11 11 11 11	108
77 77	93	88 88 (LM)	8	11 11 11 11	135
77 77 77	17	88 88 (LM)	10	11 11 11 11	138
77 77 77	25	88 88 (LM)	15	11 11 11 11 11 11	149
77 77 77	47	88 88 (LM)	24	12 12 11 12	111
				14 14 4 7 8	112

Index of First Lines and Titles

(First lines are in ordinary type. Titles are included in *italics* unless they match the opening line of the text.)

First line or title	Psalm
A blameless life	26
A depth of satisfaction	1
A hallmark and a signature	8
All day long	71
All the earth, exalt the King	47
All you have created	104
Almighty Lord, your saints are glad	140
Always faithful	143
Ample grounds for praise	81
Anointed by tranquillity	23
A patchwork quilt of platitudes and lies	12
Appointed by the Lord	110
As Lord of all	110
A steadfast heart, a blameless life	26
A welcome guest	5
Be gracious to me, Saviour God	57
Be joyful, be skilful, and come with new songs	33
Be my refuge	62
Beyond this age	49
Both extremes	30
Bring to God your new, best songs	96
Bring to the Lord a song of joy	134
But a house	127
But if these trials	44
By foreign streams we sat and wept for Zion	137
By the inmost longings	66
Can a house be built to last	127
Captive birds fly free	124
Celebrate with gladness	95
City of God	87
Come, celebrate with gladness	95
Come from nations far and wide	47
Come into God's presence to worship and sing	135
Come, one and all, from near and far	49
Come, praise the Lord, all you nations	117
Come with a song of joy	100
Come with newly-written anthems	98
Come with thanks to offer to the Lord	107
Constantly with us	46
Contend, Lord	35
Dare we forget	78
Day and night I cry to you	88
Dream come true	126
Dwarf the heavens	57
Endless care	107
Enthroned in heaven	115
Extol the God of justice	9
For help in troubled times we pray	20
For justice	58
For the honour of our King	45
For your delight	21
Fresh encounters with your grace	28
From age to age, Lord, you endure	90

First line or title	Psalm
From a well-intentioned heart	17
From my aching inner turmoil	77
From the depths my soul cries out	130
Give honour to the Son	2
Give praise to the Lord	33
Give thanks to God, for he is good	136
Glad to honour you	140
God before me, God beside me	16
God beyond earth's finest treasure	16
God ever present	53
God has given us a King	72
God is good to all his people	73
God is our refuge, God is our strength	46
God, my ever-present refuge	71
God my Refuge and my Rest	62
God of might, I call to you	54
God, save me from this onslaught	59
God to whom I bow in worship	109
Good to all his people	73
Great God whose presence we have known	75
Great is the Lord, renowned among his people	76
Great Judge of all	94
Guide my thoughts tonight	4
Have mercy on me, loving Lord	51
Have mercy, Righteous One	4
Heartfelt unity	133
Help in troubled times	20
Helper and Deliverer	70
Here is the lamp	119a
Here is the route laid out for us to follow	119a
His love endures	136
His presence and his throne	48
Holy God, I cry for mercy	143
Holy is he!	99
However great the treasures life affords	121
How glad I was to meet my friends	122
How good it is to give you thanks	92
How good it is to share	133
How lavishly you give	65
How long, Lord	79
How safe it is	91
I bring my prayer	17
I call to you, my Rock	28
I delight in your decrees, Lord	119b
I entrust myself to you	56
If I should close my heart of hearts	14
I flourish in your presence, Lord	52
If only	14
I gladly trust	25
I love you, Lord, for you answered me	116
In a strange land	137
In full integrity	41
In the day of looming trouble	70
In troubled times	86
In your presence	84

First line or title	Psalm
I will praise the Lord forever	34
I will sing a song of triumph	129
I will sing your mercies, Lord	30
I will stand with God's people and pour out my praise	111
Jerusalem!	122
Joy comes to those who have trusted you, Lord, for salvation	112
Know that the Lord	100
Let all creation's wonders	148
Let alleluias ring	148
Let all the earth bring joyful songs to God	66
Let all the earth rejoice before the Lord	97
Let every door be opened wide	24
Let every nation bow in godly fear	99
Let me walk with you	101
Let the King be crowned	72
Let this honour	149
Let us exalt our King	145
Like dogs	59
Like them	106
Listen, Lord, to my complaint	64
Lord, do you see the evil in the world?	94
Lord God, have you rejected us	74
Lord, hear my prayer and guard my life!	86
Lord, hear the lonely sufferer's cry	22
Lord, hear your people's cry	79
Lord, I am determined: I shall praise my King	108
Lord, I approach your sanctuary	15
Lord, I ask you to be gentle	38
Lord, I dearly love your presence	84
Lord, I gladly trust in you	25
Lord, listen to my cry	61
Lord, make my prayer a sacrifice	141
Lord, show me how to count my days	39
Love enduring evermore	89
Love will be our song for ever	89
May God be gracious, granting us his favour	67
May God, our God, arise	68
Mercy, God! My foes pursue me	56
Morning, noon and night I plead	55
My chosen home	27
My focus all my days	61
My God, I long to meet you	42, 43
My God, I pray for help	5
My Lord, you have examined me	139
My refuge is God: why, then, should I flee	11
My Rock and my Refuge, take note of my cry	31
My soul, this sorrow	42, 43
My trust and triumph	63
Never holding back	108
No lofty dreams are mine	131
No peril we encounter	121
Not in anger but in love	6
Nowhere can rival the city of God	87
Offerings born of brokenness	51
On your mercy	130
Our hope, our refuge be	90

First line or title	Psalm
Out of life's quagmire I was rescued	40
Out of the grasp of death	116
Peace in your promise	69
Praise the Lord	146
Praise the Lord for ever	34
Priestly devotion	135
Prisoner of despair	88
Refuge and Rock, Shield and Deliverer!	18
Remember, Lord	74
Rescue me, God: the floods engulf me	69
Revealing timeless wisdom	19
Robed in majesty, he reigns	93
Royal Master	45
Save me from my enemies	64
See life as a psalm	150
Shepherd of the chosen flock	80
Show your face	80
Sing of Yahweh's splendour! Gather to rejoice	149
Sing out, my soul, in gratitude	103
Sing praise to the Lord, you people of grace	150
Sing, sing of unfailing love	103
Sing to the Lord with gratitude and wonder	105
Sing with every kind of music!	81
So firm and sure, those ancient hills	125
Song of triumph	129
Speak, Lord, and let us hear again	83
Still I am protected	54
Such tales are heard from long ago	44
Surely, Lord	109
Take courage, you saints	31
Take up your servants' cause, Lord	35
Teach me, Lord, your compassion	41
Tell what he has done	105
Thankful hearts	50
The cry goes up	82
The cry is heard from heaven	82
The finest fruit	1
The glorious King	24
The heavens proclaim God's glory	19
The honour, Lord, is yours	115
The kindness of his face	67
The lonely sufferer	22
The Lord who reigns in Zion	48
The mighty God addresses all creation	50
The privilege of praise	96
The righteous have a lifelong aim	37
The thrill of God's forgiveness	32
The timeless certainties of love	60
The voice which shakes the earth	29
The weight of guilt	38
The whole of life	128
The wisdom of the past	78
They will not be forgotten	111
This is our God	76
This is our prayer	112
Through and through	139
To count my days	39
To stand for truth	120

First line or title	Psalm
Unfailing love! The Lord our God is good	118
Unfailing purpose	138
Unless the Lord had stood with us	124
Unless you help me	13
Unnumbered miracles of mercy	40
Unseen footsteps	77
Unshakeable for evermore	125
Weaving reverence and excitement	98
We owe our thanks to you, Lord	65
We turn our eyes to you	123
We worship you, whose splendour dwarfs the cosmos	104
What faithfulness, Lord, and what love you have shown!	138
What flaws and failures	15
What was it but the presence	114
When anxious thoughts assail my mind	13
When battle clouds	144
When David had a longing	132
When Israel left Egyptian days behind	114
When loneliness and anguish fill my days	102
When the pressures I encounter	3
When times of desperation come	60
When trouble looms on every side	10
When we face impending warfare	144
When you brought the captives home	126
Who dares imagine a life spent without you?	53
Who else but you	75

First line or title	Psalm
Whoever fears the Lord	128
Why do the nations rage	2
Will our rulers stand for justice	58
Wisdom whispers in my heart	36
With God my Saviour as my light	27
With hallelujahs honour God	147
Within my heart a desert lies	63
Within the busy rush of life	23
Within the holy place	134
Within the shelter of the Lord	91
With resounding alleluias	146
With such contentment	131
Words that only wound	12
You are my Refuge and Deliverer	7
You are my security	3
You know my way, the path I have to take	142
You know the pressures I endure	120
Your chosen servant	132
Your endless love, your mighty acts	106
Your favour rested on this land	85
Your gifts exceed	21
Your gracious judgements	119b
Your love surrounds me	52
Your love will be my song	101
Your majesty is splendid, Lord	8
Yours is the verdict	7
Your sovereign hand	102
You servants of the Lord	113